A FOR ADOPTION

The experience of adoption—both adopting and being adopted—can stir up deep emotional pain, often related to loss and early trauma. *A For Adoption* provides insight and support to those families and individuals facing these complex processes and challenges.

Drawing on both a psychoanalytic, theoretical framework and first-hand accounts of adopters, adoptees, and professionals within the adoption process, Alison Roy responds to the need for further and consistent support for adoptive parents and children, to help inform and understand the reality of their everyday lives. This book explores both the current and historical context of adoption, as well as its depiction within literature, before addressing issues such as conflict in relationships, the impact of significant trauma and loss, attachment and the importance of early relationships, and contact with birth families.

Uniquely, this book addresses the experiences of, and provides support for, both adoptive professionals and families. It focuses on understanding rather than apportioning blame, and responds to a plea from a parent who requested "a book to help me understand my child better".

Alison Roy is a Consultant Child and Adolescent Psychotherapist and the professional lead for child and adolescent psychotherapy in East Sussex Child and Adolescent Mental Health Services (CAMHS). She is also the clinical lead and co-founder of a specialist adoption service called AdCAMHS.

Tavistock Clinic Series

Margot Waddell, Jocelyn Catty, & Kate Stratton (Series Editors)

A FOR ADOPTION

An Exploration of the Adoption Experience for Families and Professionals

Alison Roy

Routledge
Taylor & Francis Group

LONDON AND NEW YORK

First published 2020
by Routledge
2 Park Square, Milton Park, Abingdon, Oxon OX14 4RN

and by Routledge
52 Vanderbilt Avenue, New York, NY 10017

Routledge is an imprint of the Taylor & Francis Group, an informa business

British Library Cataloguing-in-Publication Data

A catalogue record for this book is available from the British Library

Library of Congress Cataloging-in-Publication Data

Names: Roy, Alison, 1966- author.
Title: A for adoption : an exploration of the adoption experience for families and
    professionals / Alison Roy.
Description: Abingdon, Oxon ; New York, NY : Routlegde, 2020. |
    Series: Tavistock Clinic series | Includes bibliographical references and
    index. | Identifiers: LCCN 2019051223 (print) | LCCN 2019051224 (ebook) |
    ISBN 9780367439484 (hardback) | ISBN 9780367439477 (paperback) |
    ISBN 9781003006633 (ebook)
Subjects: LCSH: Adoption.
Classification: LCC HV875 .R69 2020 (print) | LCC HV875 (ebook) |
    DDC 362.734—dc23
LC record available at https://lccn.loc.gov/2019051223
LC ebook record available at https://lccn.loc.gov/2019051224

ISBN: 978-0-367-43948-4 (hbk)
ISBN: 978-0-367-43947-7 (pbk)
ISBN: 978-1-003-00663-3 (ebk)

Typeset in Palatino
by Swales & Willis, Exeter, Devon, UK

For Gordon, Catherine, and Ewan. For with you, my heart has found a home.

CONTENTS

SERIES EDITORS' PREFACE

Since it was founded in 1920, the Tavistock Clinic—now the Tavistock and Portman NHS Foundation Trust—has developed a wide range of developmental approaches to mental health which have been strongly influenced by the ideas of psychoanalysis. It has also adopted systemic family therapy as a theoretical model and a clinical approach to family problems. The Tavistock is now one of the largest mental health training institutions in Britain. It teaches up to 600 students a year on postgraduate, doctoral, and qualifying courses in social work, systemic psychotherapy, psychology, psychiatry, nursing, and child, adolescent, and adult psychotherapy, along with 2,000 multidisciplinary clinicians, social workers, and teachers attending Continuing Professional Development courses and conferences on psychoanalytic observation, psychoanalytic thinking, and management and leadership in a range of clinical and community settings.

The Tavistock's philosophy aims at promoting therapeutic methods in mental health. Its work is based on the clinical expertise that is also the basis of its consultancy and research activities. The aim of this Series is to make available to the reading public the clinical, theoretical, and research work that is most influential at the Tavistock. The Series sets out new approaches in the understanding and treatment of psychological disturbance in children, adolescents, and adults, both as individuals and in families.

A For Adoption brings to life the "collaborative and generous sharing of resources and ideas" that lies at the heart of its approach to working with adoptive children, young people, and families. While the voice that leads and shapes the book is Alison Roy's own, she includes two "'companion contributors", John Simmonds and Robin Solomon, whose chapters not only contribute different professional perspectives but also attest to the inspirational and fruitful working relationships developed with Roy over many years. Roy's own chapters also bring in the diverse voices of numerous professionals, young people, and adoptive parents in a truly collaborative endeavour. It is perhaps no surprise, then, to find that the model of the service Roy leads and describes—AdCAMHS, for Adoption Child and Adolescent Mental Health Services—is one that aims to "work across disciplines, support partnerships, join agencies together to work collaboratively with adoptive families, and straddle public and private divides".

A For Adoption begins, after an Introduction that helpfully sets the scene, with literary voices. In its evocations of the enduring power of stories of adoption, drawing on Philip Pullman, Frances Hodgson Burnett, and J. K. Rowling, among others, the first chapter reminds us "that the adoption experience is, and has always been, familiar and central to the making of families since time began" and that thinking about "our parents' histories and those of their parents, and so on, have already played a big part in forming who we are". Weaving her accounts of these fictional stories together with reflections on the importance of story-telling for children who have been adopted, Roy argues that "the most positive and resilient adoptive families that I have encountered are ones where there has been a concerted effort to weave a common thread between the two story lines, creating a living tapestry that records the lives of both the adoptive and the birth families."

John Simmonds, of CoramBAAF and the Kinship Care Alliance, then contributes a chapter giving the historical context for adoption since the first Adoption Act of 1926. He traces in the next chapter both the legislative framework and the key issues surrounding adoption and its rationale, from the need in the 1920s to address the disruption to family life caused by the First World War and the 1918 flu epidemic, through shifting social attitudes to single motherhood, to the current focus on abuse and neglect. He argues that this evolving history indicates "a powerful set of forces at work that determine and drive what is a basic belief in all societies—the belief, rights, and expectations of both parents and the wider community that children should be brought up within their family of origin and if not by the parents, by the wider family". He relates this to the rise and fall of the idea of the "clean break" and describes a newer "definition of adoption as a process that means the coming together of two family trees—blended in in some form and separate in others". Yet he also raises the significant question of the support needed for the child "to recover from what is a highly anxiety-provoking task involving significant degrees of loss and grief and uncertainty".

There follow three chapters by Roy on clinical perspectives, and on parents' and young people's perspectives. The first two of these chapters succeed in keeping the child's experience centre stage while bringing to life some of the pressures felt by, respectively, professionals and adoptive parents. Roy then describes social work colleagues feeling themselves "always in the firing line" and laden with the projections of children, birth and adoptive parents, and professional networks. The chapter looks at the adopters' perspective and makes clear what a collaborative approach the book has been: Roy describes parents, aware of her writing the book, wanting her "to make it clear just how difficult it can be for adoptive parents and to emphasize their need for a 'life-line' when times are especially hard". In the next chapter, the young people themselves then bring alive the conflicts experienced in adolescence; here Roy emphasizes particularly what she describes as the "call of the wild". This painful and complicated phenomenon sees adopted children experience, as young adults, "the 'draw' of their birth family like they have never experienced it before", often producing an urge, metaphorically or literally, to run away. Here, too, the importance of story-telling becomes palpable. One young person, interviewed anonymously by Roy to inform the chapter, uses the interview to explain herself to her adoptive parents: "to say 'sorry' to her parents for running away. . . . She explained, that she runs because she wants to find her way back to her birth mother and continues to feel like a 'lost' baby who wants and needs her 'mummy'."

The book then turns, directly and indirectly, to Roy's AdCAMHS service in Sussex, starting with a chapter by Robin Solomon on the professional couple, the consultant, and the outside world, which draws on her role as a consultant to Roy's service in the first years of its development. At the heart of this engaging chapter is its account of the need for "arms-around" holding and containment, for teams and networks as well as for children and families. Solomon advocates the presence of a third, "the consultant, who can have an eye on the professional and organizational contexts . . . above the surface"—in this case, someone who "can view the world of adoption and the policies and structures that surround it, while simultaneously keeping the other eye on the re-enactments of dysfunctional couples projected from the children and families." Someone, in other words, "who can observe what is going on 'below the surface'".

This is followed in the next chapter by two discussions about AdCAMHS, one each by Roy and by Solomon, which introduce the model and its aims in detail. In the first discussion, Roy describes the model as a "psychoanalytically informed adoption service", encompassing NHS clinicians and social workers employed by the county council, with the aim that the two groups be facilitated to work together "as partners". Solomon then focuses on her consultation to the professional couple (including Roy) who set up the service, suggesting that the aims of the model be extended to supporting professionals' relationships with each other.

In next chapter, Roy turns back, as it were, to the birth parents: both to the impact of adoption on the birth parent left behind and the experiences of adopted adults thinking about their original families. She juxtaposes an anonymous professional's experience of trying to support a mother who had had eight babies taken into care, and who wanted to keep hold of the ninth, with that professional's own personal experience of contacting her own birth mother as an adult. These moving, interwoven accounts bring home the trauma of loss for adults giving up, or obliged to give up, their babies, along with the impact on children, "suddenly severed from each other" and burdened with the deep distress of being separated, an experience that stays with them "potentially for the rest of their lives".

Roy then turns to the notion of "continuity of care", here helpfully reframed as the more human idea of being "side by side". While acknowledging that professionals and services "cannot ever hope to compensate [children] for all the loss that they have experienced", she makes the case that they can "positively influence a child's life through building . . . consistent relationships [with them and their families] that can provide the continuity and nurture required to help redress the balance". And at the end of the book she concludes that investing in relationships is central to growing healthy families, organizations, and communities. This absorbing and compelling volume, with its "group portrait" of family and professional life, will undoubtedly make a very significant contribution to that process.

ACKNOWLEDGEMENTS

For Adoption has been a long time in the making, and I am most grateful to Routledge and the Tavistock Series Editors, Margot Waddell, Jocelyn Catty, and Kate Stratton, for bearing with me. Jocelyn has patiently maintained her enthusiasm and steady support during the process of bringing the book together, and Margot has continued to believe in me and the book, helping me to trust that one day it would really happen. She has been a source of inspiration over many years, since the early stages of my training as a child psychotherapist, and I have learned much from her about how to remain thoughtful and curious, particularly in my work with risky adolescents.

At times, *A For Adoption* has felt rather like an unruly adolescent, but it has challenged and delighting me in equal measure. I would therefore like to thank all the young people, parents, and colleagues who have contributed their thoughts and experiences to this book, either through quotes or interviews, helping to make it a more personal account of the adoption experience. To those who have regularly entreated me to "write it all down", I can only say that without your insistence and confidence in me, I would never have considered taking on such a project in the first place.

Special thanks go to my two "companion" contributors, John Simmonds and Robin Solomon, who have been model professional partners in their collaborative and generous sharing of resources and ideas. John was one of the first people to encourage me to write about my work with adoptive families, so that the opportunities and demands might be better understood in the public and political domain; he has been an inspiration and a source of wisdom and support throughout my professional "adoption journey", as well as in the writing of this book. Robin, on her part, has provided sensitive and wise counsel over the years. She has been an oasis of calm, offering me a place of nurture and shade away from the heat of working within a highly pressurized public-sector landscape, showing me that relationships do matter, despite the emphasis (at the time of writing) on targets and performance data. She has continued to be a source of inspiration and wisdom and has consistently grounded me in theory and practice (and common sense), which has enabled me to do what Bion (1987) described—to think under fire.

I would also like to thank: Sussex Partnership NHS Foundation Trust and East Sussex County Council, and local managers within those organizations; Mike Wright and Claire Padgham, who have accompanied me in building a psychotherapeutically led service for adoptive families in East Sussex; and all those working alongside me in the AdCAMHS team. I owe a great deal to my professional partner, Jane Drew, who has modelled good relationship-based practice for well over a decade, and who has been unfaltering in her ability to be "reflective and brave", as a colleague once described her. She has weathered many storms metaphorically and literally beside me, in work with families and young people and in adolescent group sessions and woodland camps. Thanks, too, to the Looked After Children Mental Health Services (LACMHS), who forged the way for a consultation approach to working with mental health in partnership with social care professionals in East Sussex and who have generously shared areas of good practice.

Finally, I would like to thank my husband, Gordon, for his support and impressive capacity to stay awake through long chapter readings, tolerating those late nights and early mornings, but also for remaining interested in my writing and for encouraging me to keep going; and our children, Catherine and Ewan, who never cease to amaze me with their insight and honesty, and for reminding me that loving and playful relationships are central to being human, helping to put many of our task-focused adult preoccupations into perspective.

> "I could really use a book to have to hand, to help me understand my child better . . . a book that could help me in my role as an adoptive parent . . . but one that isn't set out like an 'idiot's guide' by clever, well-meaning experts. I need a book which acknowledges just how complicated it all is and recognizes that I'm also an expert. I do know my child best—even when I'm really struggling . . ."

(Adoptive parent)

ABOUT THE AUTHOR AND CONTRIBUTORS

Alison Roy lives in Sussex with her husband and two children. She is the professional lead for child and adolescent psychotherapy in the Child and Adolescent Mental Health Services (CAMHS) in East Sussex and the clinical lead and co-founder of AdCAMHS, a specialist adoption service. Within these roles, she provides direct therapy and group work for children, young people, and their parents, as well as training, consultation, and supervision for professionals across both CAMHS and children's services. She also works in private practice with adults, adoptive families, and adolescents.

Before training as a child psychotherapist, she trained as an arts journalist and went on to edit and produce a youth magazine. She later founded a community arts project called Generation Arts Project (GAP), harnessing the creative potential of challenging and vulnerable young people.

More recently, Roy was the Director of Media and Communications for the Association of Child Psychotherapists (ACP) and the editor of the *ACP Bulletin Magazine*. She also regularly contributes expert pieces about children's mental health in the press and in various other mainstream or specialist publications.

Contributors

John Simmonds, OBE, Director of Policy, Research and Development at CoramBAAF, has worked in the area of social work, adoption, and children and young people for over 45 years. He was a social worker in Hampshire and Camden, and Lecturer and then Senior Lecturer in Social Work and later appointed to Head of Social Work Programmes at Goldsmith's College, University of London. In 2000, John joined the British Association for Adoption and Fostering (BAAF), now CoramBAAF, as the Director of Policy, Research and Development. He has written and edited a number of publications, including *Good Practice Guidance: The Role of Special Guardianship* (2011) and *The Child Placement Handbook: Research, Policy and Practice* (co-edited with Gillian Schofield, 2009). At the time of writing, he is also Chair of the Kinship Care Alliance. In 2015 he was awarded the Order of the British Empire (OBE) for services to children and families.

Robin Solomon was a consultant social worker at the Tavistock Clinic, where she held senior roles in both clinical work and teaching. She is now an independent consultant, a senior fellow of the Higher Education Academy, and a Trustee of the Centre for Social Work Practice. She has worked as a trainer and consultant in a number of social care and mental health settings and has provided training and consultation for post-adoption support social workers and practitioner leads specifically for East Sussex.

The Author and Publisher would like to thank the following for the permission to use copyright material:

Adele Adkins, Dan Wilson: Extract from "Someone Like You" (2011), reprinted by permission of Hal Leonard Europe Ltd on behalf of the writer.

J. M. Barrie: Extracts from *Peter Pan* (Penguin Popular Classics, 1995), reprinted by permission of Great Ormond Street Hospital Children's Charity.

Robert Del Naja, Grantley Marshall, Andrew Vowles, Tracey Thorn: Extract from "Protection" (1994), reprinted by permission of Hal Leonard Europe Ltd on behalf of the writers.

Philip Pullman: Extracts from *Northern Lights* (1995) and *The Amber Spyglass* (2000) reprinted by permission of Scholastic Ltd on behalf of Philip Pullman.

Introduction

When I first started writing *A For Adoption*, I was responding specifically to the issues I encountered in my work with adoptive families as well as those raised in consultations with social workers. However, I have since altered my focus and have responded to a more personal plea from families: to write something that could be "accessible and companionable" for them too, validating their experiences and potentially giving them more of a voice within the public domain.

A For Adoption is therefore not an academic book as such and is written to be inclusive. It is a book for adopters, for adoptees, for those considering adopting, and for those who support adoptive families—in fact, for anyone who is interested in or is directly connected to adoption.

The book begins by looking at how stories have described and shaped our lives throughout history and how central the adoption story is within society. It is interesting how these ubiquitous and ancestral stories or tales about adoption continue to be reworked into contemporary novels, films, and works of art. I have started the book by focusing on the fictional narratives about the adoption experience, but I go on to develop these themes by examining the real-life "stories" of those who have been adopted and are willing to share their "no-frills" accounts.

Some contributors have explicitly asked for their views to be included, whereas others have provided more general material and ideas. These first-hand or lived experiences, which are central to the book, come from an adopted professional, a number of adoptive parents, adopted young people, and professionals providing adoption support or psychotherapeutic interventions. I have not identified anyone personally except three colleagues: John Simmonds, Director of Policy and Research at CoramBAAF, who has written a chapter about the political and historical context of adoption, examining the challenge of forming a family from a family that is broken; Robin Solomon, Senior Fellow at the Higher Education Academy and a Trustee of the Centre for Social Work Practice, who talks about the central role of the professional couple in helping the adoptive family to manage the challenges of the outside world; and Jane Drew, my professional partner in the specialist adoption service, called AdCAMHS, that we co-founded in Sussex. Jane has worked alongside me over the years to forge a partnership approach to working with adoptive families. All three colleagues talk or write in an impassioned way about the importance of relationship-based practice in adoption support work.

I am most grateful for the input and wisdom they and others have generously given over the course of writing *A For Adoption*, but also to those who have been willing to be interviewed and have given their permission for their personal experiences and reflections to be included in order to help others on their adoption journey.

While a book can never replace therapy, learning about the experiences of others can help adoptive families to feel less isolated and better understood—restoring connections with others and offering the opportunity to become part of the wider adoption community. Within this community, there is an eagerness to share not only first-hand experiences but readily available literature and on-line resources documenting approaches to mental health disorders and difficulties relevant to adoption.

Many of the parents I work with are keen to find out all they can about what would help them and their children manage the big challenges they face. However, there appears to be much less written outside these parent forums, about the more personal experiences of adoption and how hard it can be to lead a "normal" family life. The middle section of the book is dedicated to this aspect of adoption, where combined voices provide a sense of the wider adoption community—drawing from the shared experiences of children, young people, their parents, and the professionals who work alongside them.

Adoption is an emotive issue affecting everyone to a greater or lesser degree. Within extended families, wider friendship groups, or gatherings of work colleagues, there will be an adoptee or someone who has become an adoptive parent. Adoption therefore touches the lives of

many—even politicians and leaders, who will have their own perceptions of adoption and what adoption support should look like.

Some are well informed about the issues facing adoptive families such as Edward Timpson CBE, a previous Minister of State for
Children and Families from May 2015 to June 2017 and former Chair
of the Children and Family Court Advisory and Support Service
(CAFCASS). He made no secret of his personal interest in adoption and
was instrumental in establishing the Adoption Support Fund (ASF).
There are different views on how beneficial the fund has been for
adoptive families and for the services working with them, but, when
it was introduced, many parents were heartened that someone within
parliament seemed to be taking the time to understand their plight and
provide them with resources. Timpson himself talked openly about
how his involvement in adoption policy stemmed from his experience
of growing up with fostered and adopted "siblings" and how his parents fostered nearly 90 children and adopted 2 of them. In a *Guardian*
interview (Rustin, 2014), Timpson reflected on how these relationships
shaped his life.

> I've obviously thought about this a lot and I've come to the conclusion
> that I wouldn't be the children's minister and I wouldn't have gone
> into family law if my parents hadn't fostered.

He also confessed that he initially struggled to understand why he had
to "share [his] mum with other children. . . . There's never a moment
even now that I go round to her house and there isn't a child there."

There have been other historical political responses to children in
need that have been less well informed or well-intentioned and have
even caused significant harm. In the post-war period, child migrants
as young as 3 years were shipped to Canada, New Zealand, the former
Rhodesia, and Australia. This practice continued into the 1960s and early
1970s, and it took decades for politicians to "notice" what was happening, the catastrophic consequences, and to put a stop to it. Over 7,000
children were sent to Australia under assisted child migration schemes,
and it is well documented that many of these "adopted" children were
brought up in children's homes, institutions, and orphanages or placed
in unregulated foster care. Because the majority of these children who
arrived overseas were placed in group "homes", they did not have
parents or parental figures to protect and nurture them. Instead, they
experienced neglect and abuse, and some were even treated as unpaid
workers and servants while in "care".

On 16 November 2009, the Australian Government formally apologized to "Forgotten Australians and child migrants" on behalf of the
nation, and in February 2010, British Prime Minister Gordon Brown

added an apology for Britain's role in sending thousands of children overseas. Interestingly, it was social workers like Margaret Humphreys CBE, OAM, from Nottinghamshire, who in 1987 set up the Child Migrants Trust (CMT; https://www.childmigrantstrust.com) and challenged politicians about this practice, holding them to account, along with others.

Adoption has also featured in the press and broadcast media in relation to children and young people's mental health, as the correlation between adoption or being in care and having mental health difficulties becomes better understood. It makes perfect sense that those who have experienced early-life trauma such as significant loss, abuse, and neglect are more likely to have a mental health diagnosis later in life.

A report commissioned by the Department for Education, *Beyond the Adoption Order: Challenges, Interventions and Adoption Disruption* (Selwyn, Wijedasa, & Meakings, 2014) looked in detail at post-adoption order disruption rates. What they found was that, although the rates for disruption appeared to be very low, behind the figures were other kinds of breakdowns in family relationships and significant difficulties, such as those encountered in the teenage years. These problems, which were more common than disruption figures had indicated, presented a very different side to adoption and raised questions about the level of support provided for adoptees and their adoptive parents.

At the time of writing this book, there is considerable interest in children and young people's mental health, with proposed reforms linked to health, education, and social care. However, despite these proposed reforms and promise of additional resources, many adoptive families say they continue to feel invisible or neglected when it comes to mental health services or special educational provision. They also argue that they do not get the same level of support that foster carers are entitled to and can be left very much on their own, "holding the baby".

The level of public interest and media coverage about children's mental health and the plight of some adoptive families portrays a complex picture, but this still offers little in the way of answers or provision of longer term resources. These accounts can also be presented without all the contextual information, which adds to a lack of understanding about the real issues for adoptive families. To make matters worse, services that have previously acted as "safety nets" within the community are dramatically declining, and the remaining services are no longer equipped to provide the early intervention and timely support to vulnerable children and young people who have high levels of distress and disturbance or who exhibit challenging behaviours.

On top of all this is the evidence that there is growing pressure on children in school settings to "succeed" even from a very young age—a situation that could potentially fuel fears of further rejection for those who have already encountered "failure" through attachment disruptions, family breakdowns, and the negative perceptions of others. Unrealistic expectations placed on children who are not in the right state of mind to achieve their target grades can only add to their belief that they will never reach the longed-for elusive "success" and may also cause them to doubt their own potential as they become aware of the lack of investment in their future.

A significant number of adopted children may also have the additional difficulty of having been exposed to substances in the womb (see chapter 9), affecting their brain development and their emotional or intellectual capabilities. These difficulties, like foetal alcohol spectrum disorder (FASD), are rarely visible at the time of adoption but create significant complications for the child as he or she grows up. Families and professionals who are familiar with these problems say that more could and should be done to support these children and their parents more effectively.

Clinically there has been a response to a growing awareness that children born from parents who themselves have mental health disorders may have experienced early attachment difficulties and could also go on to develop other diagnosable mental health problems. There have therefore been a number of new or enhanced treatment models and specialist assessments (all with their inevitable acronyms) that have been designed to treat these disorders. However, the parents I have spoken to insist that although they are mostly grateful for the support and treatment they have been offered, ultimately they feel that they require much more than any single intervention, however appropriate, attractive, measurable, and accessible it appears to be.

Unfortunately more longer term, consistent, and multi-professional support is too often not available, even when the complex difficulties seem to be affecting every area of a child's life. This lack of support, covered from different perspectives within this book, can lead to fatigue or burnout and engender feelings of despair or powerlessness—feelings that can then be transferred onto professionals. When this happens, families may well find themselves also being transferred, "passed on", or even closed to services where interventions or programmes of treatment have not (on the face of it) improved matters. This is especially hard for families who have invested hope in these services. I have heard from families who are full of praise and respect for the professionals who support them, but I have also been told of many accounts where families have suffered rejection, isolation, and despair—experiences that are all too common for adoptive families.

In 2013, I co-founded a specialist adoption service in Sussex called AdCAMHS (Adoption CAMHS), with my social care colleagues, in response to the number of adoption cases coming through CAMHS, which required a more specialist and specific package of support. Although I cover the development of this project in chapter 7, it is important to acknowledge here that some of the presenting difficulties we see do not always improve significantly. What can change, however, through a more integrated or joined-up approach across services, is the level of understanding about these issues, leading to a greater commitment from professionals to work more closely and in partnership with adoptive parents and families wherever possible.

I have also learned first-hand (and am still learning) how even highly trained, experienced (and well-meaning) professionals like myself can further exacerbate the experience of isolation for families who are referred to our services. Sometimes this happens through the way we communicate (our labels and our "lingo") but also in our rush to find solutions, or by oversimplifying very complex issues, without having fully understood the difficulties. We can also be guilty of not creating enough space to reflect on our own encounters with adoptive families and our responses to them.

As busy and beleaguered professionals, we can become so concerned with our own capacity to manage that we fail to take in or appreciate the impact on parents and their wider family of caring for some of society's most compromised and vulnerable children, at great cost to themselves. Failure to notice this affects our practice and can seriously limit the protective function of the professional network surrounding an adopted child. This is where supervision and reflective practice plays a key role, and I shall explore how this aspect of our work can help to shift things when they start to feel "stuck", before the fatigue sets in. This is a topic covered by Robin Solomon in chapter 6, where she describes how "teams deprived of a containing experience, or where reflective opportunities are denigrated, can often feel either deadened or explosive."

This book, therefore, seeks to address these difficult themes in greater depth, while encouraging professionals to incorporate more self-reflection in their work. This is an approach that is underpinned by a psychoanalytic theoretical framework. It provides a secure base for exploring what cannot be consciously understood even among professionals, but it also encourages us to be curious about how our decisions and interactions in the present are influenced by our experiences from the past.

Being able to reflect on our interactions and processes through providing a thoughtful and containing presence for adoptive families is vital if we are to help them manage high levels of frustration and anxiety and to weather times of despair and desperate loneliness. It also means developing the capacity, resilience, and willingness to make sense of the overwhelming nature of early loss and separation. For good post-adoption support work will involve opening up honest and non-judgmental conversations with parents about the challenges of adoption and how we might tackle some of these challenges together.

When it comes to adoption, then, very little is straightforward—but, in writing this book, I hope to encourage a greater understanding of the real issues, so that those immersed in the experience will feel less alone. I hope, too, that it might serve as a helpful guide for those who commission adoption services or who will be making decisions about what resources should be made available at a local or national level, leading to more "joined-up" conversations with adoptive families and professional networks about what is needed. For it is only when we can do this that we can fully understand what John Simmonds from Coram-BAAF refers to as "complex dynamic processes . . . central to experience of adoption" (2008).

Amelia Earheart, American aviator and avid explorer [1897–1937], said:

You haven't seen a tree until you've seen its shadow from the sky.

A For Adoption, then, is an overview of adoption, seen from different perspectives in order to provide a fuller picture. It creates an opportunity for the reader to focus on the more intimate and personal experiences of adoption without losing sight of the wider social and political landscape. In the words of an adoptive parent:

"What I first set out to do has transformed into something far more complicated and demanding than I anticipated. Nevertheless—it has (mostly) been a rich and rewarding experience."

CHAPTER ONE

Adoption stories: beginning at the beginning

Tell them stories. They need the truth. You must tell them true
stories, and everything will be well, just tell them stories.

Philip Pullman, *The Amber Spyglass* (2000)

Stories about adoption are embedded in our social psyche and
folklore and remind us that the adoption experience is, and
has always been, familiar and central to the making of families.
Perhaps, too, there is something in all of us that relates to the experience of feeling lonely and "different", searching for a place where
we can find a home and escape from the cruelty and harshness of
life by being welcomed and accepted into the bosom of the family
or community.

In this chapter, I explore how stories can help all of us understand adoption, while encouraging us to think about what shapes our
identity—from our very first moments of life within the womb, through
to adulthood. For whatever we believe about the point at which a
human life begins, it is becoming increasingly clear, through numerous research studies looking at genetic influences, that our parents'
histories, and those of their parents, and so on, have already played a
big part in forming who we are (Douet, Chang, Cloak, & Ernst, 2013).
It is not possible to be clear about how much a child's identity and
quality of attachments is influenced by environment and how much is

down to genetics, but there is a growing body of work that points to the probability that it is both. Graham Music's book *Nurturing Natures* (2017) covers this subject extensively, as does Allan Schore's work on the interactions between genetic influences and environmental risk factors (2000, 2012).

Because there is so much about the beginnings of a human life and the development of the brain that remains a mystery, I have selected stories that will, I hope, be helpful in enhancing our understanding about birth, parenthood, and adoption. Stories are central to the process of learning about what it means to be human, regardless of age, gender, birth place, or race. They can also illuminate some of the more inaccessible themes that crop up within the adoption experience, such as being severed from birth parents, a predicament that has been central to the plot of countless novels, fairy tales, and films.

The task of finding one's true identity without the parents who conceived us is fraught with difficulty, and even some of the fictional portrayals of such a loss can be upsetting. I remember as a child watching Walt Disney's early animation film *Dumbo* with my family, and how we had to hastily exit the cinema because my youngest sister became inconsolable at the point where the baby elephant suddenly became separated from his loving and protective mother. These heart-wrenching themes that feature in *Dumbo*, and in other Disney or similar children's films, are central to traditional fairy tales on which many of the films are based. These tales, or stories, have been passed down through generations, like those rewritten by the brothers Grimm—Jacob [1785–1863] and Wilhelm [1786–1859] and by Hans Christian Andersen [1805–1875], but still hold meaning and relevance for families today.

How to survive the death or loss of a parent/parents is another related theme explored in innumerable novels and key texts, such as Rudyard Kipling's *The Jungle Book*; J. M. Barrie's *Peter Pan*; Charles Dickens's *Oliver Twist* and *Great Expectations*; Charlotte Brontë's *Jane Eyre*; Francis Hodgson Burnett's *The Secret Garden* and *The Little Princess*; Shakespeare's *The Winter's Tale*; and many more, including stories by writers like Roald Dahl, who himself suffered a number of catastrophic losses as a child.

Finding a story that helps to describe and make sense of a hard-to-digest experience can be tremendously important, not only for an adopted child or young person, but for all children and their parents. The most positive and resilient adoptive families that I have encountered are ones where there has been a concerted effort to weave a common thread between their two story lines, creating a living tapestry that records the lives of both the adoptive and the birth families.

A shared and understood narrative is equally important for professionals. Social care colleagues who place children usually have detailed information about the process of adoption and the matching of children with families, which can be helpful to other professionals seeking to support the family. They also have chronologies and backgrounds leading up to being removed, which adoptive children and young people can ask to see. However, some of these chronologies and later-life stories are full of "holes", and, despite considerable "digging", little may be known about aspects of the early history. Making sense of this experience is nevertheless important, for not having a well-documented history is part of these individuals' stories and does not exclude them from having a version of their experience that they can be comfortable with.

There will always be much that is not fully understood, for all of us, about our earliest experiences and what influences our life choices. We also need to take into account the fact that previously held views or definitions of families are changing, and that there are many different kinds or arrangements in place when it comes to parenting or raising a child. Today, the conventional and traditional concept of what makes a family has shifted, making way for a new kind of "normal". This does not mean, however, that children are any less interested in knowing where they come from or who they are connected to. What is important is that children are not discouraged from asking difficult questions, and that they are positively encouraged to be curious about themselves and why they might feel different from others.

I have often wondered about how to helpfully combine information from an adoptive family's history with the birth family's history, to provide a child or young person with a more holistic version of his life story, such as where he came from and how he came to be adopted, but also what his potential influences and triggers might be. A young person once asked me whether she should draw her adoptive family tree or that of her birth family for a history assignment in school. I contemplated with her how she might go about including both.

As far as the adopted child or young person is concerned, the not-knowing can feel like a place of shadows and secrets, adding to the struggle of making sense of his identity, especially when he may already feel that he is very different from his non-adopted peers. Most will get to a point where they (and their parents) can no longer hide behind the bright hopefulness of the stereotypical adoption "fairy tale", where a childless couple become parents and the "abandoned" child finds a loving home.

You don't have to scratch too far beneath the surface to see how powerful themes of loss and sadness are going to be pretty central to individual and family stories, despite a "coming together" as a family unit, once the adoption order has been granted. Adoption may be a new beginning—or another beginning—but new beginnings do also tend to stir up feelings left over from previous beginnings and endings.

This perspective is not intended to be negative, but the stories I have chosen do help to uncover more of the painful (truthful) realities, including the "bits that often get left out" (in one adopter's words), of the adoptive experience. These potentially more painful or "missing" bits of the experience are, however, made more bearable and hopeful for the reader (and probably also the writer) when they are contained within the creatively crafted framework of the narrated story.

Jeanette Winterson, an author who herself was adopted, writes in *Why Be Happy When You Could Be Normal?* (2011):

> The baby explodes into an unknown world that is only knowable through some kind of story . . . but adoption drops you into the story after it has started. It's like reading a book with the first few pages missing. [p. 5]

Children can usually find a way to tell us about their feelings and life experiences through play or make believe, or by the way they behave in some situations and with certain people. They will therefore have their own methods of storytelling, and some can be very accomplished storytellers. Through the medium of the story, children can access feelings and/or memories that may otherwise have been unavailable to them.

Every adoptive family member will have his or her own incomplete version of their family story—the why, when and how their family came to be together. They may not recall the same details of events as other family members, or they may hold information that others don't possess, but they will still need their individual stories to be heard and validated: only then can there be a way of sharing the story more openly and having the experience of it being meaningful or coming to life, or, at the very least, being laid to rest—through its telling.

According to Daniel Siegel (1999), a clinical professor of psychiatry:

> Our dreams and stories may contain implicit aspects of our lives even without our awareness. . . . [S]torytelling may be a primary way in which we can linguistically communicate to others—as well as to ourselves—the sometimes hidden contents of our implicitly remembering minds. Stories make available perspectives on the emotional themes of our implicit memory that may otherwise be consciously unavailable to us. [p. 333]

There is evidently a wealth of material to be found on the subject of adoption within films, literature, plays, or musical theatre productions like Les Misérables and Annie, but there are also the visual representations of adoption provided through the medium of paint or other art forms.

In 2015/16, the Foundling Museum, London, put on an exhibition entitled, The Fallen Woman, featuring paintings and art instillations documenting the traumatic experiences faced by unmarried women in the nineteenth century. These women were ostracized for conceiving children out of wedlock and were all too often forcibly separated from their babies. Paintings such as The Lost Path (1863) by Frederick Walker, The Outcast (1851) by Richard Redgrave, and The Gate of Memory (1864) by Dante Gabriel Rossetti were all included in the exhibition, which provoked a flow of heart-felt responses from those who visited, particularly among women who had lost or given up their own children and those closely related to a family member who had experienced a "forced" separation. There was also a specially commissioned sound installation by musician and composer Steve Lewinson, who worked with actors to bring to life the voices of the women who gave up their babies to the Foundling Hospital. One of the organizers of the exhibition reflected on how the exhibition had affected people and what she saw as the "deep . . . trauma [which] still lies in many families".

Although policy and culture has changed since the nineteenth century, taking a child or children from one family and placing them with another is unlikely to be a straightforwardly "happy" experience, especially if the baby or child has not been relinquished willingly. There will inevitably be painful and fraught times where the loss of one family and the arrival into another is likely to be disorientating and traumatic— indeed, some children never really recover from this.

Adoption histories may include the factual details of early separations, but the intense emotional distress these cause can never be fully appreciated by professionals placing a child or by their new adoptive parents. Perhaps this is where stories can paint a more accurate and universal picture of the adoption, from the rich and varied pallet of emotional experience: a picture that can be viewed from a number of perspectives.

In my work with adoptive families and with organizations working with them, I have found that some of the most painful and traumatic stories or disclosures can be hard to take in at a first sitting. There can be an initial understanding, but the fuller picture can only take shape through the process of sharing ideas and formulating a plan together, acknowledging the need for a supportive environment in which it can be possible to hear the distress and pay attention to our own responses to what we are hearing. Unlike a painting, hearing real stories about real children may also require specific action to be taken in order to protect a child from harm. This means that thinking and reflecting serves to inform our decisions but does not prevent us from having a clear plan of action. In my experience, when there are stories that cannot be discussed or heard, the risk increases, and I have witnessed how some families with painful (his)stories are "bounced around" the system. As one social worker explained, "these families are passed from pillar to post . . . it's like everyone thinks that someone else should deal with the high level of distress and concern".

In some high-profile cases, risks and documented concerns appeared to have been ignored or glossed over, as with Victoria Climbié [2 November 1991 to 25 February 2000], who was tortured and murdered by her guardians. Her death led to a public inquiry, which resulted in changes to child protection policies and procedures in the UK. Right up to her death, she had been in contact with universal children's services and her local church. In a public inquiry, headed by Lord Laming, it was noted that professionals failed to act, despite being in position to do so, and that if someone had taken action and engaged with her story about the abuse she was suffering, her death would have been prevented. This is an extreme example of how distress and trauma can become apparently "invisible" when a particular story is too painful to process. Having an awareness of why this can happen, and therefore creating the space to reflect on the full story and what needs to be shared, is important, then, in order to learn from such tragedies.

In reality, it is difficult to know exactly what has occurred in the first hours, weeks, months, years of a child's life, but as he or she grows up, more of the information that has been hidden or "stored" away can begin to surface.

> "Even though I now know what happened—it doesn't feel like it was me there—it's like it wasn't real. But the anger—the anger is real!"
> (Young person—talking about abuse he suffered from his stepfather)

These fragments of thoughts or early memories may gradually show themselves over a long period of time, but they can also take the form of extreme physical responses to certain situations or people. Some parents have described to me how events from their child's past can suddenly surface and seem to come "crashing into our family life, like lightning". They feel that they are in the midst of an intense emotional storm, which understandably leaves them reeling. These strong reactions are meaningful, despite being disturbing, for they can provide clues about past experiences. However, parents and professionals on the receiving end of these reactions will require good supervision in order to be able to hear, bear, and piece together the story and, in doing so, begin to integrate disconnected or "lost" parts of the self.

Robert Louis Stevenson, in *Treasure Island* (1883), describes the powerful influences of the past on the present landscape:

> This Grove, that was now so peaceful, must then have rung with cries, I thought: and even with the thought I could believe I heard it ringing still. [p. 234]

Another young person, who was able to recall much of her childhood, explained how she had developed "a secret self" in order to distance herself from her distressing history.

> "I can't be honest with anyone about my birth family or my adoption . . . so I feel like my story has been 'locked up' inside."

She had created a false persona in order to protect herself and others, fearing that those close to her would struggle to cope with the more distressing aspects of her history. By presenting a more palatable and well-edited version of her life, she could feel accepted and "normal", whereas a true or "truer" version of her life would, she felt, have been too painful for everyone. She did, however, admit that if she had been able to be more authentic, "it would have been better in the long run".

> "I have found that it's best just not to talk about it, because when I told a friend about how I felt, it ended up going around the whole school. In my new school, I haven't told anyone [about my adoption]. What's the point? I can't even tell my parents that I think about my birth mum—even though I never really knew her. . . . They [my adoptive parents] would get sad if I told them, they might even reject me."

On hearing this, I was reminded of the story of Rapunzel, as told by the Grimm brothers (Grimm & Grimm, 1812). There are different variations of the story, but the central theme is of a young woman who was trapped in a tower, all information about her birth parents or their origins kept from her. She had been conceived after her birth mother ate vegetables, or lettuce, or fruit (depending on the version of the story) from the garden next door, which belonged to a witch. Eating the "forbidden" fruit cured the mother of her infertility, but the high price to pay was relinquishing her new baby girl, Rapunzel, to the witch. Rapunzel had, therefore, been taught that hiding was central to her survival. However, her yearning to be found and to live her own life made it possible for her to discover the truth and find the means to reach out to others for help, such as growing exceptionally long hair and singing her story from her tower.

Adopted children and young people often describe how confused and conflicted they feel. Some say they feel "stuck" in a life they haven't chosen while nevertheless being filled with love for and gratitude towards their adoptive parents; others harbour a deep resentment about being removed from their birth parents or long-term foster carers, in order to complete a new family, knowing that their first family has been broken. There are also others who feel that their adoptive parents are "perfect" for them, and they can't imagine being anywhere else.

However, even those who feel very much at home can describe the same feelings of confusion about their identity and struggle to be authentic—to know where they "fit" in society. The fact that children were not able or permitted to make their own decisions about their futures can also create tension between them and their adoptive parents.

Jeanette Winterson, again, in *Oranges Are Not the Only Fruit*, writes about other selves or lives not realized, existing in parallel to the life lived and a hankering after what might have been. She reflects on how very different her life would have been had she remained with her birth mother.

> I have a theory that every time you make an important choice, the part of you left behind continues the other life you could have had. [Winterson, 1985, p. 164]

This is complicated for parents who want their adopted child to feel at home and secure in the knowledge that he or she is loved. They are frequently mystified or can, understandably, feel betrayed by their child's desire to make contact with their birth parents—especially if these birth parents were abusive or unprotective.

To put this experience into context, it is important not to underestimate the instinctive and primitive need a new-born baby has for his or her birth parent—for to begin life without the one whose voice and heartbeat they have become familiar with, the person who knows them completely and who can filter the outside world for them, is potentially catastrophic. When a birth parent is absent, lost, or unavailable, the infant has no one to help process the pain, and he or she begins to close down emotionally. This can happen even in the early hours or weeks of life and will therefore have already had a significant impact on a baby or young child before he or she is adopted. This unfulfilled desire or yearning for the birth parent seems to remain, even if it appears dormant, and can therefore surface at various points in the child or young person's life.

This yearning, or what others have described as a deep sense of loss, is hard to explain.

There are very rare adoptions where the unborn infant will have heard the adoptive parent's voice, and both infant and adoptive parent therefore have a little bit of an understanding about each other before beginning their journey together. I would stress, though, that this is very rare indeed, and most will come together pretty much as strangers. There is, therefore, a vital part of the child's early experience that has been lost or remains inaccessible to adoptive parents as they seek to piece together their child's history. The wished-for happy fairy tale can therefore begin to feel more like a tragedy, as the significant experiences of loss rooted in infancy continue to surface. One adoptive parent reflected on the sadness of not being there at the beginning of her children's lives, but also referred to her experience of adopting as a "comedy of errors".

Professionals (affected by their own vulnerabilities and potentially difficult histories) do understand what parents interpret as "errors", in that they may also struggle to gather up all the important information about the child's history and to know what is most relevant to share with adopters. They will also have their own stories and vulnerabilities and struggle with being viewed as the "baddy" in the story—the one who has to "bear the brunt of everyone's frustrations and disappointments", as one social worker put it—when their intention had been to bring joy and to do good. This is why it is important to give all the main "players" or characters, including professionals, their say in this combined telling of the adoption story as the book unfolds.

Shakespeare writes, in a *Comedy of Errors*:

A heavier task could not have been imposed
Than I to speak my griefs unspeakable.
[Aegeon to Duke of Ephesus; *Comedy of Errors*, I: 1.]

A children's novel that, I think, beautifully illustrates key themes relating to the experience of adoption is *The Secret Garden* by Frances Hodgson Burnett (1911). It narrates the physical and emotional journey of discovery for Mary Lennox, the central (adopted) character, by using the metaphor of the garden.

Mary was abandoned and neglected—a lost and forgotten little girl who had been emotionally abused and uncared for by her parents since her infancy. Although the story is written for children, it addresses very complex and adult themes, including death, romantic and filial love, and the impact of a significant bereavement and catastrophic loss on the development of the child's personality. It also explores how loss can affect an adult's capacity to care for a child.

The story begins with a description of Mary as being unwanted, where the adults around her have forged or "forced" her identity as an "unlovable" child. She is described early on in the book as being "the most disagreeable-looking child ever seen." Born in India, where she is lonely and neglected, cared for only by her Ayah, who also has little time for her, Mary knows that her parents do not love her, know her, or understand her. But then they suddenly die and leave her physically and emotionally alone—completely abandoned.

> During the confusion and bewilderment. . . . Mary hid herself in the nursery and was forgotten by everyone. Nobody thought of her, nobody wanted her and strange things happened of which she knew nothing.
>
> She only knew that people were ill and that she heard mysterious and frightening sounds.

Mary is discovered by an army officer, who is startled to find a young child alone in such a desolate house. This part of the story resonates with the "real" histories I have heard and read about in my adoption-focused work, relating to a child's early experiences before they are taken into care or adopted. Hearing "mysterious and frightening sounds", beyond the child's comprehension, is a strong thread running through many background histories or chronologies, and features in the telling of many a child's version of their early life story.

As already mentioned, protective adults act as filters for children, processing events and frightening encounters or experiences for them, in order that they can be digested. When the main caregiver is not able to do this, or wilfully visits further traumas on the child, a child's natural need for others and his healthy desire for intimacy is seriously affected. So, too, is his impression of the world as a place to explore and to be curious about.

> "It is the child no one ever saw!" exclaimed the man, turning to his companions. "She has actually been forgotten!"
>
> "Why was I forgotten?" Mary said, stamping her foot. "Why does nobody come?"

Mary showed some character and appropriate resentment towards her abandonment, but she has no means of transforming her hateful and "hated" feelings into something or someone who can aid her growth and development. In this respect she was very much like the "Mistress Mary Quite Contrary" from the nursery rhyme, a phrase that other children taunted her with.

If we go back to the beginning and think about the earliest experiences for a baby, that of being in the womb, then it is possible to see how a child like Mary begins to experience herself as unloved or unwanted. In this "merged" place where mother and baby are joined, the feelings and experiences of both can be transferred or communicated from one to the other. These may well be positive, forging a bond between parent and infant, needed for survival in the outside world, but they may also be uncomfortable and distressing. Mary seems to have "known" that she had never been loved and that she had arrived in the world feeling unwanted. However, by using the metaphor of the garden, Hodgson Burnett is able to germinate the dormant seed or need (the yearning previously mentioned) for relatedness in Mary, which finally begins to grow when it is noticed and nurtured.

The psychoanalyst Michael Balint, who wrote extensively about ways of relating to others and how these have been influenced by our infantile experiences, described the environment for the baby in the womb as an "area of creation".

> According to my theory, the individual is born in a state of intense relatedness to his environment . . . prior to birth, self and environ-ment are harmoniously "mixed up" . . . in this world there are as yet no objects, only limitless substances and expanses. [Balint, 1968, p. 67]

Mary, despite her deep distress and acute awareness of her plight, maintains the capacity to seek out life and to return to the "area of creation" in her mind. This inner life appears to be hibernating and stays very well hidden in the early pages of the book, but it gradually surfaces when Mary begins to risk being curious about and interested in life and being alive. It is as if she is growing "little shoots" of feel-ing for others coupled with her budding awareness of the beauty of the natural world.

Adoption for Mary, then, provides a reprieve from neglect and trauma, but she has to endure a lonely journey, taken in by an unknown uncle (Mr Craven), who lives in England, who himself is in hibernation emotionally, since the loss of his beloved wife. His own loss has caused a deep depression in him—a desolation of the soul and a state of mind that leaves him preoccupied and absent from the children in his care. Perhaps this bereavement triggered memories of a former or primary loss for him, for he appears to be deeply attached to his loss and is unable to recover from it.

Mr Craven's son, Colin, who was born shortly before the death of his wife (who, interestingly, had a fatal accident in the garden), is aban-doned by his grief-stricken father and, like Mary, is left alone emotion-ally, effectively placed "in care" and attended to by servants.

Meanwhile Mr Craven wanders the world in search of meaning, but his own experiences of unresolved and sudden loss have prevented him from claiming his son and addressing his own pain. With the arrival of Mary comes another reminder of the loss and the secrets that have had to be maintained in order to avoid such emotional pain. Colin is to be kept separate from Mary, hidden away in the depths of the mansion where he and now Mary live—a "home" that has become more like a prison to Colin, rather than an environment facilitating exploration and the delight of discovery.

In my experience, it is not uncommon for the painful, traumatic histories of an adopted child to trigger unresolved emotional wounds or sensitivities for the adoptive parent. I have even worked with parents who have a strong desire to keep this pain and "contaminating" loss away from themselves and the rest of the family and attribute it all to the child. Like Mary, some adopted children have their bedrooms in separate "wings" of the house, or up in the loft, as if to keep them at a safe distance.

> "Well here you are! This room and the next are where you'll live—and you must keep to them. Don't you forget that!" It was in this way that Mistress Mary arrived . . . and she had perhaps never felt quite so contrary in all her life.

Despite this separate and confined existence for Mary, she learns that there is more to life than being confined within such a limited and "dull" environment, and, with Martha's (one of the servants') help, she begins to discover the new and sensual world, beyond the restrictive walls of the house—a world of "other" and difference outside herself. Fortunately, her life instinct is stronger than her deadening need for control over others, and she begins to explore this outside world symbolized by the different kinds of landscapes or gardens she encounters in her "fresh air walks". She also keeps bumping into the gardener, Ben Weatherstaff, who gives her a few home truths.

> He began to dig . . . driving his spade deep into the rich black garden soil, while the robin hopped about . . . he jerked his thumb towards the robin. "He's the only friend I've got."
> "I have no friends at all," said Mary. "I never had. My Ayah didn't like me and I never played with anyone."
> It's a Yorkshire habit to say what you think with blunt frankness, and old Ben Weatherstaff was a Yorkshire moor man.
> "Tha' an' me are a good bit alike," he said. "We was wove out of the same cloth. We're neither of us good-lookin' an' we're both as sour as we look. We've got the same nasty tempers, both of us, I'll warrant."

As she takes in Ben Weatherstaff's honest appraisal of her, coupled with her interest in the natural world, she begins to ask herself important questions about how she might understand and embrace life more fully.

The experiences of change, loss, and then growth and happiness become more important to her. It is at this point that she begins to converse with the robin, who perhaps represents a curious little part of herself, one that is beginning to stir—to come to life. This side of herself has been well buried, like the key to the secret garden, which the robin shows her, when she is ready to make good use of it. It is also like the soil in the garden, neglected and uncultivated, but now gradually germinating seeds and growing all manner of shoots that are pushing their way through the darkness and into the light.

> The robin hopped about, busily pecking the soil. . . . Mary thought his black dewdrop eyes gazed at her with such curiosity. It really seemed as if he was finding out all about her. The queer feeling in her heart increased.

Mary is ready to learn about herself but this is a new experience for her as she takes Ben Weatherstaff's comments to heart, wondering if indeed she is "nasty tempered". She feels "uncomfortable" about this, but it does mean that she has found the key to unlock the door to her true feelings and her inner world.

> Mistress Mary went a step nearer to the robin and looked at him very hard.
> "I'm lonely," she said.
> She had not known before that this was one of the things which made her feel sour and cross. She seemed to find it out when the robin looked at her and she looked at the robin.

Daniel Stern, a distinguished child psychiatrist, psychoanalyst, and developmental psychologist, writes about the infant as a social human being from the very beginning of life, born with the capacity for attracting communication from others.

> [E]mergent relatedness assumes that the infant from the moment of birth is deeply social in the sense of being designed to engage in and find uniquely salient interactions with other humans. [1985, p. 235]

These self-reflections, despite being uncomfortable for Mary, allow her to risk knowing further "truths" about herself, being prompted by her new-found desire for life and to be social. She is now eager to grow and wants to recover from her traumas and maladies, and it is at this point that she discovers she is not as alone as she had feared. She is surprised to find that she has the capacity to connect with others, a state of being not encouraged by her birth parents, who, instead, taught her to "close down" emotionally and keep others "shut out". Through the continued acceptance from Martha, but also the much-needed challenge from those close to her, a new hopefulness and self-awareness emerges.

Consistent caregiving, combined with healthy challenge, is a winning combination for child rearing, but this is far from straightforward and something many parents struggle with. This is even more complicated for adoptive parents who are keen and even encouraged to be, as one adopter explained, "endlessly compassionate". It can be quite complicated to muster a robust but appropriate challenge to a severely traumatized and deprived child. This does, however, need to be part of the parenting "offer" when it comes to building a secure attachment with adoptees—or what is often referred to as "tough love". This is not the same as being punitive or intrusive, and it comes from place of real awareness and a deep understanding of the child and his or her needs.

The secret longings from Mary's infancy—her yearning to be loved and understood and to belong—are reawakened through the challenge she receives from characters like Ben Weatherstaff, as well as the love and attentiveness of Martha, making it possible for her psychological garden to spring to life. She is, understandably, delighted to find shoots forging their way through the weed-choked soil and immediately clears a space for them to emerge and blossom.

Once Mary has discovered the secret garden, she finds other "lost" things or people—like Master Colin, who is hidden away in a secret wing of the house, believing himself to be an invalid—a belief that Mary wastes no time in challenging. Mary also meets Dickon, a boy who is vibrant and healthy, with a strong attachment to his mother (Susan Sowerby). At this point in the story, it is as though Mary has tapped into a rich vein, supplying her with the elixir of life. She becomes more joyful by the minute about her wonderful discoveries and new friendships, spurred on by Colin, who is also "waking up", as if from a deep sleep, with the arrival of spring. The long winter, for the two children, has finally passed!

I remember the words of an adopted child who slowly came to life through his therapy session. He suddenly found that he could create scenes three-dimensionally using toys or Play-Doh, whereas previously he had only drawn on the chalkboard, believing that nothing was lasting and every connection would be "wiped away". During one of these creative moments, his eyes opened wide, as if he were seeing me for the first time, and he exclaimed, "My head feels like it's getting bigger and bigger, it's like my brain hurts with it all, you need to understand, it's like every thought leads to another and then another!"

Susan Sowerby, Dickon's mother, who herself is at ease with the natural world, provides good nurture to all the children in her care and those who touch her children's lives. She instinctively knows what Mary needs and intercedes on her behalf with Mr Craven, so that when Mary asks him for a piece of soil—a little garden (but cannot tell him it is his secret garden, and that she has found the key)—he agrees.

Mary's observation of Mr Craven is keen: she notices that his disability is of his own creation and also recognizes how unhappiness has altered him.

> He was not ugly. His face would have been handsome if it had not been so miserable . . .
>
> What an unhappy face he had! His black eyes seemed as if they scarcely saw her, as if they were seeing something else, and he could hardly keep his thoughts upon her.
>
> "I forgot you." he said. "How could I remember you? I intended to send you a governess or nurse or someone of that sort, but I forgot" . . .
>
> "I am too big for a nurse," said Mary.
>
> "And please—please don't make me have a governess yet."
>
> "That was what the Sowerby woman said," he muttered.
>
> . . . "She knows about children," said Mary.

Mr Craven explains that Mrs Sowerby has entreated him to notice Mary and think about her needs, so Mary feels emboldened to respond:

> "Might I," quavered Mary, "might I have a bit of earth?"
>
> . . . Mr Craven looked quite startled.
>
> "Earth!" he repeated. "What do you mean?"
>
> "To plant seeds in—to make things grow—to see them come alive,"
> . . .
>
> "A bit of earth," he said to himself. . . . When he stopped and spoke to her, his dark eyes looked almost soft and kind.
>
> "You can have as much earth as you want," he said. "You remind me of someone else who loved the earth and things that grow. When you see a bit of earth you want, . . . take it child and make it come alive."

I have witnessed how a child coming to life psychologically can inadvertently help to restore colour and purpose to a stuck or despairing adult. That is, these opportunities can be possible when an adult is willing to learn and change, despite his or her desire to defend against emotional pain. Professionals such as social workers do, however, need to be able to distinguish between a parent who is consumed by his or her own needs and difficulties and therefore resents (and may even sabotage) the healthy development of his or her child or children, and a parent who has become fatigued or misguided but wants to help and support his or her child through these difficulties. The latter parents need help in order to show that they have the propensity to be happily "surprised" by their child, as opposed to being continuously "absent" or preoccupied.

Mary's birth parents had no interest in meeting her needs or understanding her, and they only desired for her to kept away from them so that they didn't have to have contact with her. However, Mr Craven kept himself away from his son for fear that his grief and disability would negatively affect or even damage him. He also secretly believed that his own inadequacies had already permanently damaged his son. He was, however, fairly easily persuaded to attend to the needs of the children in his care, and in this adoption story he happily discovered his potential as a parent, despite his previous failings. Parents who cannot be mindful of their children and who prioritize their own needs and desires over their children's can be harmful to them. Capacity to change is a key factor in social work assessments of parents whose children have been or are at risk of being removed, as well as for potential adopters.

> While the secret garden was coming alive and two children were coming alive with it, there was a man wandering about certain far-away beautiful places . . . and he was a man who for ten years had kept his mind filled with dark and heartbroken thinking . . .
>
> But, strange as it seemed to him, there were minutes—sometimes half-hours when, without his knowing why, the black burden seemed to lift itself . . .

As his soul begins to stir, he has a dream that he hears his deceased wife's voice calling his name. He asks her where she is so that he can come to her, and she replies:

> "In the garden," it came back to him like a sound from a golden flute. "In the garden!"

Following the dream, he receives a letter from Susan Sowerby, entreating him (again), but this time to return home, with the words:

> I would come home if I were you. I think you would be glad to come and—if you will excuse me, sir—I think your lady would ask you to come if she was here, . . .

Mr Craven does return and slowly makes his way to the garden, where he comes face to face with his son, full of physical vitality and ideas. To the children, it feels as though the father has finally come home to them.

He listens to the children as they tell him their story of how they came to life in the garden.

> The listener laughed until tears came into his eyes, and sometimes tears came into his eyes when he was not laughing.

Sadly, not every child or young person who loses their parent(s) has had the opportunity to find new parents or become part of another family. For children and young people who have spent much of their time growing up in residential care homes, the *Harry Potter* stories by J. K. Rowling, published between 1997 and 2007, can be helpful. These stories are a fictional account of how it can be possible to feel at home in institutions, just as long as there is a consistent and supportive team of adults around to provide nurture and structure. The central character, Harry, a boy wizard, is an orphan who is parented by a number of different adults. Some of these become key attachment figures for him, like Albus Dumbledore, the Principal of Hogwarts (the school where Harry lives in term time), and Hagrid, the groundsman. There are also his best friend's parents, his godfather, and others who all play their part in watching over Harry as he transitions from childhood to adolescence.

For Harry, it appears to be the combination of having access to enough trusted adults and the solidity and dependability of the physical building in Hogwarts Castle that provide a secure-enough base to help him develop his own sense of identity. In this respect, the institution becomes a real "home" for Harry, who does not really have anywhere else to go. Hogwarts as an environment can challenge him and expand his mind, but it also encourages his inquisitiveness and the courage to learn about himself and his past.

There are other malign characters in the stories who attempt to undermine Harry's positive experiences at Hogwarts, including his aunt, uncle, and cousin who are meant to "care" for him when he is not boarding. However, they don't understand him and separate him from the rest of the family by giving him a bedroom that is effectively a cupboard under the stairs. There is also the constant threat of evil hovering over Harry in the form of Lord Voldemort, the Dark Lord, previously known as Tom Riddle, an ex-student of Hogwarts. This dark presence seeks to impress Harry, control him, and lead him astray. It also hones in on Harry's emotional distress and vulnerability, intending to provoke Harry's darker and more destructive feelings. Hogwarts appears to be the right place to "hold" and motivate the conflicted Harry, with the help of wise grown-ups and highly experienced staff, who seem to know how to support him while helping him to manage his destructive tendencies. Led by Albus Dumbledore, the staff members are encouraged to be mindful of the risks and challenges surrounding Harry and his past.

These stories are a creative reminder of the crucial role that therapeutic residential settings and communities can play in the lives of older children, or young people in particular, who cannot be held or safely contained within a family environment.

At the time of writing, these kinds of communities for young people are diminishing and under threat due to a crisis in funding within social care. This means that there are fewer therapeutically run centres available to support these young people long-term, many of whom have been through numerous placement breakdowns and losses and have "given up" trying to form meaningful attachments or waiting for a significant caregiver to come and claim them. Well-managed institutions with access to education and therapy and a strong focus on community can therefore be transformative for some young people, offering them different prospects and life choices, who might otherwise end up in the criminal justice system.

"It is our choices, Harry, that show what we truly are, far more than our abilities."

[Albus Dumbledore, in *Harry Potter and the Chamber of Secrets*; Rowling, 1998, p. 333]

CHAPTER TWO

Creating a family life from a family life that has been broken

John Simmonds

I have asked John Simmonds, OBE, Director of Policy, Research and Development at CoramBAAF, to write this chapter. He has been working in the area of social work, adoption, and children and young people for over 45 years. I came across him in 2014, when my colleague and I were presenting our new adoption service as a good-practice model for working with and supporting adoptive families. This was before the arrival of the Adoption Support Fund, and we were advocating for a partnership approach to adoption support, in which organizations such as social care and mental health would work together with adoptive families. Simmonds was supportive of this model and recognized the centrality of relationships with adoptive families. As an adopter himself, he has repeatedly highlighted the complexity of dynamic processes within the adoption experience and the need for professionals to get more of a handle on this. He has therefore championed the AdCAMHS service model (see chapter 7) in a number of forums and at a policy level and has encouraged thinking around the level of complexity that adoption throws up for families and those services who support them.

In this chapter, he provides a historical context to adoption and the bringing together of a family from their separate places of both loss and hopefulness.

Adoption—parenting and family for a child where the birth parents cannot provide this on a permanent basis—has had a long history, over many generations. Establishing a legal framework and identifying and agreeing the situations in which adoption might be used is relatively recent in the UK, with the first Adoption Act coming into law in 1926. In other countries, adoption has taken a different timeline, with a specific local focus on the issues it is designed to address. Every country will design its own approach for the use that is to be made of adoption, including, usually, a legal framework. As adoption has come to include a significant international set of issues, there are both international as well as national agreements that set out the basics of adoption within a human rights framework. This will typically include the right of every child to be raised by their birth family and their birth family's right to raise them.

In the UK, the problems to be addressed by adoption have significantly changed since the first Adoption Act. The design of the original legislation was focused on the disruption to family structure that resulted from the death of large numbers of men in the First World War and then as a consequence of the flu pandemic in 1918. Ensuring family inheritance and continuity through the husband/father and the maintenance of moral and social order underpinned adopted children being treated "as though they had born in lawful wedlock".

Other societal issues, especially illegitimacy and infertility, were also addressed and again were strongly linked to the issues of social and moral order. But significant changes in the societal view of single motherhood, the legalization of abortion, and the introduction of effective contraception during the 1960s moved the focus away from these primary concerns towards adoption as a solution for children with special needs. And in later years it became the solution for those children who were experiencing or had experienced significant abuse or neglect and where local authorities and the courts agreed that adoption was in the best interest of the child, even when the birth parents fundamentally disagreed with that plan for their child.

The use of the term "broken" in the title of this chapter needs to be used with some sensitivity, as there may be heightened differences of view as to who is breaking what for whom. Through to the 1960s, the three combined issues of societal disapproval of single parenthood, the protection of marriage as fundamental to the preservation of social order, and the implied consent of the single parent to her child, typically her new-born baby, being placed for adoption with respected married couples of impeccable social standing does not imply the absence of a strong sense of coercion or disapproval for the woman who "made herself pregnant". But while generally placing a child for adoption might have been seen as the "right thing to do" at the time or the "only option available", the feelings that were often powerfully stirred up cannot be ignored. And this issue continues to be raised by some of those women who understandably see what happened to them as coercive and a scandal and as requiring a public apology.

What all of this indicates is a powerful set of forces at work that determine and drive what is a basic belief in all societies: the belief, rights, and expectations of both parents and the wider community that children should be brought up within their family of origin and, if not by the parents, by the wider family, however that is defined locally. Adoption may provide an alternative opportunity for the child where the child's family of origin cannot do this, but that does not happen without a fundamental break in what is deeply embedded as a powerful survival mechanism within the human species.

The issue for children is somewhat different. They are born into the world with a complete dependency on adults: namely, their parents, who will enable their survival through the provision of milk/food, warmth, protection, and stimulation. The process of expectation on the part of the baby and response on the part of the adult are stimulated by much more than a practical set of arrangements, as there is a deeply embedded drive with a specific focused and emotional commitment on the part of the mother and father and others to respond to the child. The primitive and powerful need of the baby to be and to become connected to those around the baby has been assertively set out through the concept of attachment, providing a language that captures the essence of what it means to be human—a part of a relational world that creates, enables, and sustains individuals in every sense of who they are and what they will become.

In the early development of adoption, with its focus on the preservation of social and moral order, the removal of a child and placement with non-related adults was thought to be inconsequential as far as the child was concerned, as it was a new beginning where the child would have no memory or any connection to the birth parents or family of origin. In fact, there was an argument by some that they did not need to know, or even that it should be kept a secret. And, from the adopters' perspective, whatever problem had led to them not having a child of their own—typically infertility—was solved through the placement of a healthy baby. They could now "move on" and put the past behind them as they became a family just like any other family with "born-to" children. This was reflected very directly in the closure of the birth records of the child, with no access being lawfully allowed until the mid-1970s.

Over the years, it became increasingly clear that the "clean-break" view of adoption was unhelpful and misleading. For those children who were "told" about their adoption or discovered that they were adopted, curiosity became a significant factor, and that might lead some individuals to search out details of their birth parents and wider family, including making direct contact with them. Curiosity might also be linked to other factors, such as a profound sense of loss—"why was I 'given-up' for adoption?" or "Was there something about me that resulted in me being rejected?"

These powerful emotional questions might also be linked to a sense of genealogical and identity confusion—"who is my 'real' family?" and "who do I look like?" or "who do I share common interests with?" There are many accounts (Barratt & Lobatto, 2016; Harris, 2006, 2012) of the personal exploration and experience of these questions and a number of research studies (Howe, Feast, & Coster, 2003; Howe, Sawbridge, & Hinings, 1992; Triseliotis, 1973; Triseliotis, Howe, Feast, & Kyle, 2005) that have explored the detail of re-connecting with the past and the impact that this then had on the individual involved. On a broader front, this has come to fundamentally change the definition of adoption as a process that means the coming together of two family trees—blended in in some form and separate in others. But, at its best, adoption results in an integrated narrative for the child/adult, the adoptive and birth parents, and their wider families. And there may be a range of issues that continue to be pressing, some of which may never be resolved.

The focus of adoption has undoubtedly changed since the dramatic drop in the 1960s in the number of "relinquished babies" available for adoption. Children with special needs, children from minority ethnic families, and children who were at risk of or had experienced significant harm through abuse and neglect became the focus. The introduction of the Children Act 1989 in England and Wales reinforced this picture, with some uncertainty as to the place of adoption at all—especially where this involved dispensing with the consent of the birth parents. The 1997 Labour government re-focused on adoption from 1998 on, with an updated legislative framework and a policy and practice perspective that emphasized the significant opportunity that adoption provided in establishing a family life for a highly vulnerable group of young children. That perspective continued with the 2010 coalition government, although there were challenges to the lawful use of adoption by the Supreme Court and the Court of Appeal, with a powerful view from the president of the Family Division that adoption should only become the approved plan for the child "where nothing else would do". The uncertainty this created for local authorities and the courts resulted in the overall numbers of children being placed for adoption dropping quite significantly. This was accompanied by a rise in the number of Special Guardianship Orders, where the child left care through placement with kinship carers—typically grandparents.

What also ran alongside this was the rise in levels of awareness of the struggles that many adoptive families were having with their children that resulted from a combination of adversities—genetic and epigenetic factors, poor early care prior to and following birth, the impact of abuse and neglect, and the uncertainty for the child that resulted from the challenge of agreeing and finding a suitable adoptive home and the child's separation from the foster carer. The likely and specific impact of these factors on the child's development is complex, but a range of emotional, behavioural, and cognitive issues have been identified and that now includes the increased likelihood of neuro-developmental issues such as attention deficit/hyperactivity disorder (ADHD), autism spectrum disorder (ASD), and foetal alcohol spectrum disorder (FASD). This has resulted in increased needs and demand for support, which has, in turn, focused on a range of interventions such as adoption-related parenting programmes, individual therapeutic help for the child, and support in relation to school. The prototyping and introduction in England, from 2015 on, of the Adoption Support Fund has undoubtedly enhanced and placed the spotlight on these support issues, although there continue to be significant unresolved areas of difficulty that put intense pressure on many adoptive families over the longer term.

The resolution of these issues and difficulties—the policy and legislative framework for adoption—is complex. There are very strong views expressed on all sides about this—on the one hand, views about a coercive and controlling State that removes children from poor, disadvantaged, and struggling parents to place them with adopters who have proved that they have the enhanced personal, social, and material resources to care for those children. On the other, there are significant concerns about the extreme vulnerability of children exposed to significant abuse and neglect, whose lives and development—and, in some cases, their very survival—are threatened. Placement for adoption is judged to be the best solution in the short and longer term, where longer term means for the rest of their lives. This is where the title of this chapter reinforces a core set of questions about "how we create a family life for the child where this has been forcibly broken."

The evolution and nature of the human species is based on its capacity to cooperate and work together to find solutions to the problems of survival on a day-to-day basis and into the future. Fundamental to this capacity to cooperate is the capacity to trust—acting on the belief that what other individuals do, say, or believe is sufficiently aligned to and supportive of one's own needs and the way that they are expressed in what we do, say, or believe in. The basis of this complex and uncertain set of processes has come to be expressed through the concept of mentalization—developing the capacity to understand what is going on in our own minds, as well as what might be going on in the minds of others (Busch, 2008; Fonagy, 2002).

The uncertainty of this process results from the fact that it is not possible to know what is going on in another person's mind—there cannot be any form of direct access to another person's mind—so it is always a process that is driven by perception and structured by degrees of experience. It can also be challenging to know what is going on in one's own mind: there are always degrees of ambivalence and/or uncertainty and the necessity to change one's mind as new information and circumstances come to light. A child's experience from birth will be critical in developing the child's capacity to "know and understand" what is going on in his own body and mind and what might be going on in the body and mind of others. This is powerfully instinctive in the early years, with the baby reaching out, through crying and bodily movement, to be fed, kept clean and warm, stimulated, and cuddled. But the sensitivity and responsiveness of the parent/carer is the primary factor in ensuring that what is offered is sensitively attuned to the baby—appropriate, timely, and focused. And that requires active parental/carer interpretation of the baby's crying and movement: making sense of what might be going on in the mind and body of the baby, something that depends on a combination of instinct and the carer's own experience of caregiving, both good and bad.

Other people—partners and the wider family—can also play their part and some of these issues will be embedded in the social structure and the beliefs and behaviour about parenting and family life that result from this. But throughout, the primary issue will the capacity of the parent/adult to make sense of and interpret what is thought to be going on in the mind and body of the baby and in the parent's own mind and body—the process of mentalization.

The immediacy of the processes for the parent in making sense of and taking action also needs a longer term perspective. Patterns of interaction will emerge in the way that the parent(s) come to facilitate and structure the child's growing sense of his connection with the world through the relationships that he makes with others. Those relationships will be significantly influenced by the child's growing capacity to make sense of what is going on in his own mind—"I trust this person", "I like this person", "I want to play with this person"—and what they think is going on in the mind of the other person—"they trust me", "they like me", or "they want to play with me". And we would expect that there will also be some degree of hesitation about this as well—especially if something happens in the course of relating which suggests a different perspective: the adult or the other child turns away or expresses frustration or disinterest.

The dynamics of the relational world have come to be articulated in depth through the concept of attachment (Bowlby, 1969), followed by the further articulation of the concept by Ainsworth into "secure" and "insecure" (Ainsworth, Blehar, Waters, & Wall, 1978), and then "disorganized" by Main and Solomon (1986). The framework of attachment sets out the primary need a young child has to establish an intimate relational pattern of interaction, as described above, that becomes the source of safety and security when the child is in need, is anxious, or is feeling insecure. Trust is fundamental to what emerges, as described above. The absence of sensitivity and responsiveness by the caregivers or their physical absence will trigger the child's capacity to protest as a means of re-engaging the primary caregivers. If this does not happen, then that protest will be amplified, and under normal circumstances this will result in a caregiver response. If it does not, then protest can turn into despair, and, over time, if that pattern persists, the child will adapt to a lower level of expectation about the availability of responsive caretakers; at its most severe that adaptation will directly impact on any expectation in the child's mind of a sensitive, responsive relational world. As much as research has come to identify the components and framework of the attachment system in humans, recent developments in connected concepts such as mentalization and reflective function have further enhanced our understanding (Cooper & Redfern, 2016; Steele & Steele, 2008).

For many children who come into care, the very worst of these processes will have influenced their development and, in particular, their experiences and expectations of an intimate, responsive set of relationships where their needs and welfare are primary. The interaction between the different components is complex but is likely to result from their parents' drug and alcohol problems, poor mental health, severe instability in adult relationships including domestic violence, learning difficulties, and poor physical health. The consequences of any of these will then interact with significant aspects of social and economic deprivation, amplifying the vulnerability of the adults and, in turn, of the child or children to further significant day-to-day life stressors. The child's experience in these circumstances is again complex to be specific about, but this is likely to have resulted in the child's major adaptation to neglect and/or physical, emotional, and sexual abuse (Cicchetti & Valentino, 2015; Teicher & Samson, 2016). And the likelihood of sensitive, responsive, and timely parenting/care resulting in the development of the child's fundamental belief in his caregiver's commitment to him and his own sense of value and trust is likely to be seriously compromised. Where a local authority assesses that the needs and welfare of the child are such that an alternative family life is required to raise the child, then adoption may be one of those alternatives—especially if the child is under 5 years and the evidence is robust that no other viable option is, on balance, available.

The adoption process is therefore an intervention with a complex set of dynamic features which results from a combination of extreme vulnerability for the child, resulting from the child's experience of adults who, because of their own vulnerability, have been experienced as preoccupied with the consequences of a set of serious stress factors that has interfered with their care of the child. And this may include the child experiencing his parents or other adults as a significant source of threat. The challenge in this arises from the generational breakdown of trust, which is fundamental to human problem solving. When humans are faced with a problem, they need to draw on a combination of prior experience suitably adapted for the specific circumstances of the present. A part of this may include a sense of needing to learn if a viable solution to the problem is not immediately available. This all suggests the fundamental importance of individuals working together to explore, identify, and formulate an agreed version of the problem and a workable solution for both the immediate and the longer term. Engaging in such a process, which in many respects is typically routine, is also a potential challenge to the feelings that an individual may have about him/herself: "Am I an idiot or a fool?". . . "Am I any good at solving problems?" . . . "What are others going to think about me if they really know how idiotic I feel?" . . . "Do I feel confident enough to ask the other person what they think or how they might solve the problem?"

Over the course of time, children will develop their own ways of identifying and resolving problems, of finding ways of working with others, of recognizing their own strengths and where they need the help of others. Although cognitive skills will come to form an important part of this, emotional regulation will form another, and, within this, degrees of confidence and trust in one's own mind and the way that it guides, supports, and enables, as well as trust in the minds of others and the way that they guide, support, and enable. If there are doubts or obstacles, then it is the lessons from the past that should facilitate the resolution of these.

But, as noted above, adoption typically operates in the context where there is an almost complete absence of any of the above. What should have started with the offer to provide services designed to help resolve the problems that stood in the way of the parents providing safe and effective care for the child will have disintegrated through the lack of engagement and evidence of change and with an escalating sense of suspicion, distrust, and blame: "You don't believe me" . . . "You don't understand me" . . . "You don't care about me" . . . "You just wanted to take my child away".

Any intent to establish joint problem solving driven by degrees of trust and openness that facilitate problem identification and problem resolution will have proved to be unsuccessful. A sense of failure may then come to pervade all discussions, and this will be revisited many times, as the local authority's plan for the child makes its way through planning and decision-making processes, including the courts. The hope that needs to drive the plan for the child will be uncomfortably set within the context of relationships that have become framed by strong feelings of blame, recrimination, and fault, leaving a strong sense that relationships between the parents and services have become irreparably broken.

Where adoption becomes the agreed plan and sanctioned by the courts, hope should come to pervade the action of professionals and services. There should be a strong sense of a new beginning for the child driven by the commitment and motivation of the adopter(s). At the same time, uncertainty and anxiety will come to play a part as major adjustments need to take place in the minds of both the child and the adopter(s). The most immediate part of this will be the disruption to the child's relationship with his current carers—typically, his foster carers—and the formation of a new relationship with his adopter(s).

For the child, it is another experience of "breaking relationships" in order to "make relationships". As a part of this, there are important questions to be answered about the support the child will need to recover from what is a highly anxiety-provoking task involving significant degrees of loss and grief and uncertainty. And as a part of this, there will be questions about the degrees of recovery for the child from earlier experiences of abuse and/or neglect. These will be multifactorial— physical, cognitive, emotional, and social, and the interactions between these. The focus on repair for the child through placement for adoption will be challenged by the reality of the past and the shadow that this casts over the child and the child's adopter(s) in the present and into the future. And the primary responsibility, once the child is placed, falls on the adopter(s) to repair and rebuild—particularly the adaptations that the child will have made in order to protect himself from the direct threats to his survival or the absence of a relational world that enables and develops his capacity to trust and engage with his own mind and the minds of others and learn from experience.

For the adopter(s), creating a safe, stable, and secure world for the child will involve the familiar issues of daily routine, a healthy environment of food, cleanliness, sleep, play, and relationships, including other children within the family. There will also be important issues on the boundary of the immediate family—other family members, nursery or school, playgroups, leisure activities with friends and neighbours, and, for some children, sibling relationships where they are placed elsewhere. With each of these, the child will need to adapt, to understand, and to become familiar with and come to develop a sense of trust in what is being offered through any of these experiences. The child will need to set aside what he was previously familiar with, and resolving loss and grief may be a part of this process. But, hopefully, this will be balanced by a sense of relief, excitement, and possibility in a more child-centred world. For the child and the adopter(s), adapting to new experiences will fundamentally involve making sense of these experiences—what is going on in their own mind and body and how this relates to making sense of what is going on in the minds and bodies of others. The shadow of the past over the present will always be significant: what was learnt from those experiences, how this was adapted to, and how they came to establish a belief in the child that the day-to-day issues of safety, security, and survival could reliably be solved.

The role of the child's parents or previous carers will have been absolutely fundamental to the way that any of this became established in the child's mind and the degree to which the child experienced them as on his side: engaged, supported, sensitive, warm, and trustworthy. And it is likely that for many children placed for adoption, their experience will have been significantly on the other side: dis-engagement, the absence of support, insensitivity, lack of warmth, and a sense that nobody is to be trusted.

All family relationships are constructed on the basis of the human need to establish an active set of beliefs that both adults and children will be actively protected through their own actions and the actions of others in order to survive through problem solving. When this breaks down, the opposite of this positive set of beliefs can become embedded in the individual in a powerfully destructive way. And where there are actions to resolve those problems through a range of interventions, they can be experienced as the very opposite of what is intended: to blame, to undermine, to create guilt, and to threaten. And this can operate beyond the immediacy of the personal world—in groups and in systems. The children's care system combines all of this, and while its own solution design might be focused on positive problem resolution, the subjective experience of both adults and children might indicate the very opposite of that. And that is so in adoption. The system and its solutions are absolutely focused on the safety, welfare, and needs of the child in the long term and, indeed, for the rest of the child's life. But the system is also focused on rebuilding a life for the child and for the adopter(s) from a life that has become significantly broken. The impact and consequences of this cannot be ignored.

They can and will determine the experience of day-to-day interactions and the way that children think and feel about themselves and others—particularly their adoptive parents, but other significant people as well. There need to be supportive, insightful opportunities to put any of this into words: to explore, to be curious, to be sensitive, and to be supportive. And these are the drivers for what it actually might mean to create a family life from one that has been broken.

CHAPTER THREE

The force of the blow: clinical perspectives

I stand in front of you, and take the force of the blow . . .
protection.

Massive Attack, "Protection"

As touched on in previous chapters, adopted children and young people can be among some of the most troubled and isolated individuals with complex needs in our society. They frequently harbour doubts about themselves and their identity and can become defined by their experiences of rejection and loss, rather than by experiences that are centred around acceptance and belonging. They may also need to express their hurt by giving it or showing it to those closest to them. It is not surprising, then, that their parents or carers so often end up also feeling lost, deskilled, and isolated, doubting their worth and effectiveness as parents.

This chapter focuses more on the role of professionals in understanding these kinds of challenges and conflicting feelings and how to manage them or come to terms with them, as they seek to support adoptive families. To illustrate this, I shall draw from clinical material taken from individual psychotherapy and group sessions, but grounded in psychoanalytic concepts. I hope, too, that this exploration will be helpful for adopters or adoptees, for although professionals such as social workers and psychotherapists do not have to live with the big, day-to-day struggles, they are still grappling with similarly painful and complex issues, but from a different perspective.

Psychoanalytic psychotherapy with adopted children, young people, and their parents can provide a valuable insight into why a child or young person presents or behaves as he does. One of the reasons for this is that child psychotherapists have undergone a lengthy training, rooted in the observation of babies and children and their key relationships. Another is that it is an approach that specifically emphasizes the importance of building a secure therapeutic relationship with the child or young person, in order to help him feel more able to access areas of difficulty and vulnerability. The strength of this relationship should not exclude other key attachment figures, but it can enable the child to gradually open up and trust those who have become safe adults in his life. This will then facilitate a piecing together of aspects of the child's experience, so that the past can inform the present, even if it seems that big "chunks" of the life story have been lost along the way.

Bessel A. van der Kolk, a psychiatrist and an expert on developmental trauma, has written specifically about how the body remembers, even when the mind has apparently "forgotten". In *The Body Keeps the Score: Brain, Mind, and Body in the Transformation of Trauma* (2014) he talks about the need for courage in approaching this work:

> As long as you keep secrets and suppress information, you are fundamentally at war with yourself. . . . The critical issue is allowing yourself to know what you know. That takes an enormous amount of courage. [p. 233]

In her famous song, "Someone Like You", the singer Adele describes the pain involved in sustaining relationships and how love can "last" but can also really "hurt". This is not just the case with romantic love—it can be very relevant for relationships within families. The general assumption is that "blood is thicker than water", as the saying goes, meaning that family members will always stand by each other. However, the fact that a large number of children cannot remain with their birth families is proof that this is not always the case. Being part of a family that falls apart can be painful enough, but when children are separated from their birth parents, there is a fundamental and potentially life-changing loss to absorb. The hurt and shock that children feel affects them deeply and can create lasting problems for them in the area of relationships for years to come.

These children, like Mary in *The Secret Garden*, may well choose to close down psychologically or push others away whenever they start to get close, in an attempt to protect themselves from the threat of additional losses. This situation makes it difficult for their adoptive parents and other potentially protective adults to reach them. Some may also harbour a secret desire to return to their lost birth parents—even if they know that that environment was unsafe.

Nearly all the young people I have worked with or have interviewed for the purpose of this book described how they felt they were trying to manage a complicated set of emotions within themselves all the time. Put simply, they feel as if they are divided or split between the way they feel about their biological or birth family and their current (adoptive) family. They almost always want to protect their loved ones from their past traumas but, in doing so, find that they start to lose touch with their formative experiences, which could provide them with clues to their difficulties and challenging behaviours in the present.

Most say that they have experienced comfort and reassurance from their adoptive parents but that they have been left with a residual terror of abandonment originating from earlier losses. They also describe having a genuine worry about the power of their birth family to contaminate their meaningful relationships in the present.

For those who have had a number of placement breakdowns or changes and other early life traumas, the perceived threat of rejection feels even more intense. There is a need for constant vigilance, and the individual affected exists in a state of heightened anxiety.

"I feel that I am living under a shadow. I constantly have doubts about my self-worth, fearing that one day I will be rejected again or, worse, I will become like my birth parents who everyone sees as 'bad'. Then I will be lost from those I care about."

(Young person, age 15 years)

Margot Waddell (1998), psychoanalyst and consultant child and adolescent psychotherapist, writes about the centrality of relationships for personality development and how our early relationships prepare us for later life disappointments and frustrations:

The capacity to develop is very much dependent . . . on the different degrees to which it is possible to tolerate frustration and absence. [p. 197]

One young woman I worked with, A (age 17 years), remembered fragments of what it was like living with her birth parents, who had neglected and abused her. However, she found that the detail and feelings that "belonged" with these fragments were somehow missing. She perceived that these details relating to her early childhood experiences had been "mislaid", just as she herself had felt "lost" or not thought about—that is, until she was later "found" by her adoptive parents. She was clear that her lost (mislaid) experiences were continuing to cause her "a whole lot of trouble", and therefore she bravely wanted to face her past, learn about her birth history, and attempt to "lay it all to rest" by asking to see her old social care files, which contained some of this information.

This process of learning about her past turned out to be far less straightforward than she could have anticipated and caused an initial downward spiral in her state of mind. She did, however, slowly begin to articulate to her therapist and her life-story worker (a professional like a social worker or a therapist, who gathers all the information to be found about past and present and works with children and parents to create an understandable version of their story) how her childhood experiences had affected her capacity to form meaningful relationships. She explained that she had instinctively "known" what was the cause of this difficulty in her history but had needed the right support in order to "go there".

For so much of her early childhood, A had felt alone and afraid and had therefore needed to exert control over every new situation and potential connection with others, in order to manage any kind of "normal" life. She also insightfully surmised that, because she had had no one to turn to in her early childhood to help her make sense of these experiences, she had simply learned to forget them. A pattern of forgetting had continued into her adolescence, for whenever she felt fearful or anxious, she found that she couldn't "think straight" and had to find a way to "escape" from her feelings. She did this through running away, or by seeking out situations where she could access substances or other means of avoiding or deadening her feelings.

Bessel van der Kolk reflects on this difficulty with thinking and feeling, when an individual has previously experienced significant trauma and distress:

> Psychologists usually try to help people use insight and understanding to manage their behaviour. However, neuroscience research shows that very few psychological problems are the result of defects in understanding; most originate in pressures from deeper regions in the brain that drive our perception and attention. When the alarm bell of the emotional brain keeps signaling that you are in danger, no amount of insight will silence it. [van der Kolk, 2014, p. 64]

With a growing self-awareness, A started to use her sessions to meander around these so-called fragments, until on one occasion she felt something shift. She seemed more confident in the knowledge that her adoptive parents and social worker (and her psychotherapist) were all interested in helping her understand her fears, which she herself had linked to her past traumas. She indicated that she was afraid but was more curious (able to think) about her history. Her psychotherapist noticed the shift as A started to reflect on her childhood without "shutting down" emotionally.

A talked about her birth family home where she had lived up until she was 4 years old: the garden, the TV, and even the smells coming from the kitchen. As she spoke about the inside of the house, making her way in her mind to the bedrooms, she wrapped her arms tightly around herself and shivered. She was shocked to find that she was feeling cold and noticed that she was physically shaking, despite the warmth of the day. As she "held" herself, she recalled a memory of being small, cold, and unable to sleep—having no bed covers to snuggle into. Her cold feelings, she said, were "jumbled up" with her feeling afraid, a fear that also related to memories about the abuse she had suffered as a young child with her birth family. She was understandably upset but also amazed that her body had helped her to remember something significant. In subsequent sessions she started to explore why she felt she was being what others had described as "demanding" in her relationships, and her constant need to feel safe and warm and to be held especially tightly.

The role of psychotherapy in working through these kinds of difficulties is key. Hindle and Shulman (2008) described the importance of psychoanalytic psychotherapy with deprived children, like those who have been adopted.

> [A] psychoanalytic perspective—with its focus on the inner world, and on emotional and unconscious processes—can contribute to thinking, planning and practice of all those involved in adoption. [p. 1]

Historically, society has chosen to look on the bright side of adoption, and many prefer to focus on the "happy ending". However, although we are becoming more aware of the complexities surrounding the adoptive experience, the harsh truth about this for so many parents and children is that it is far more painful than they ever imagined it would be.

For adopted children or young people who had spent the first few weeks or, in some cases, months of their life being cared for by a team of professionals, such as nurses, rather than by a known and familiar parent figure, there are other complications. The infant may have been premature due to exposure in the womb to alcohol or opiates or other substances, and the nurses who provided the care in the infant's earliest hours after birth came and went with their changing shift patterns. This version of care, therefore, provided little opportunity for the troubled and suffering infant to bond or risk connection with others. He or she would have likely been in intense physical and emotional pain but would have had to make do with the (mostly) functional care provided, in order to survive.

After weeks of waiting, when the infant has almost given up on being claimed, an adult (such as a foster carer) may well have been identified to provide more consistent care and parenting for the infant. But for little ones who have already experienced the most traumatic and significant loss imaginable—the loss of their birth parent—this new experience of one-to-one care is difficult for them to manage. They will struggle to cope with the intense contact and level of intimacy and may take a good while to recognize and accept their new caregivers. Over time, they may begin to risk forming meaningful attachments with their consistent caregivers. However, these can be pretty shaky for a good many months and potentially years.

Imagine, then, the scenario, after a year or so, of the baby or toddler being separated again from his trusted caregiver(s) and "handed over" to another virtually unknown adult or couple. All the familiar sounds, smells, and tastes are gone—even the toys he has become familiar with may be left behind. The tentative connection that had been hard won between child and carer is also lost, along with the part of the child who had just started to trust his familiar adults. And yet, despite this traumatic loss and disorienting turn of events, the child will be expected to settle into his new home, with more new parent figures, without too many complaints.

Any child in this position, who has already experienced overwhelming losses and changes at such a key point in his development, will be likely to rebuff (in a number of ways) the well-intentioned efforts of adopters to reach him. The child may even be too shocked to receive the love that has been "saved up" by parents longing for a child. Some children also recall that their previous, trusted carers or "parents" had become upset and distracted when these new adults (potential adopters) arrived, adding more weight to the sense that they had been forcibly removed (again).

It is painful to think about how the world can change in an instant for a young child and how it can become completely unfamiliar again as he loses touch with so much of what has defined him. Children may resist for a long time all that is new, including affection and food (which often gets vomited or spat out). Sometimes these children become poorly and listless, and they cannot or will not sleep. They seem to be always waiting for someone to realize their mistake and return them back "home" again, or else waiting to face another experience of being "lost".

Eventually, a child reaches a point where he understands that he is not going back "home", but the part of him he left behind often remains lost. When such children are older, some can articulate how they remember a point when they decided never to fully trust anyone again. For these children and young people, there is a survival need to be constantly vigilant—ready for the day when the next new people will arrive to take them away from all that that they know and have grown to love.

If we take all these experiences and feelings into account, it is not surprising that professionals, too, get caught in the "cross fire", finding themselves on the receiving end of very powerful feelings relating to loss. One social work colleague described the shock she felt when she started working with adoptive families and how she felt that she was "always in the firing line".

In order to help professionals understand these experiences better, reflective practice and good supervision is key: in other words, finding a way of working that allows for the difficult and most painful feelings to be expressed and thought about. This has become more accepted in social work practice and specialist mental health teams, but it has its roots in psychoanalytic theory. However, there are so many competing demands on services that it is often not possible to make space for this valuable experience, or it may be viewed as a luxury rather than an essential part of the work. There may also be other reasons why reflective practice does not happen as readily as it might, even though thinking with others about our work can help us to understand experiences such as being "in the firing line" or taking the full "force of the blow". It is also not always possible to reflect, especially when we as professionals are feeling stressed or anxious, but it is important to make sure that there are opportunities to mull over our work and to pay attention to our feelings. Even if we can't be reflective in the moment, the factored-in space to debrief after difficult sessions or visits is key to remaining healthy at work.

Sigmund Freud, in his *Studies on Hysteria* (1895d), wrote about what we now think of as *transferred* feelings (or *transference*) from patient to analyst. He later developed the concept of countertransference (1910d), where the transferred feelings and how we *counter* them or work with them can significantly influence the therapeutic work. Others took hold of these ideas and developed them, such as Wilfred Bion (1962a, 1962b), an influential British psychoanalyst, who wrote about the importance of thinking and how distress and trauma affects one's capacity to reflect. He himself experienced at first hand the catastrophic shock and distress of fighting in the First World War, and he was also one of the first psychoanalysts to treat patients with serious mental illnesses or "psychotic states".

He highlighted the distinction between *having* an experience and *learning from it* (1962b). Bion also understood the importance of gaining a deeper understanding of processes and experiences stirred up through the therapeutic relationship—and an opportunity for the most difficult or *unthinkable* thoughts to be reunited with the thinker.

Many of Bion's theories grew out of his direct work with patients, but he also offered inferences on mother–baby interactions where the mother, or caretaker, receives or metabolizes the baby's expressions of powerful feeling, whether positive of negative, thus making it possible for the baby to understand and eventually to think about those feelings herself. This Bion thought of as a "model of the mind".

The most helpful and widely understood model is that of the *container–contained*—for example, where the parent as the container holds or contains the thoughts and projected feelings of the infant until the infant become ready to think for herself. This process of "containment" as defined by Bion (1961, 1962b), when applied in a psychotherapeutic or supervisory setting, can lead to greater self-awareness and capacity for reflection, enabling practitioners to understand and moderate even their most "reactive" responses towards the families with whom they work.

Waddell (1998) emphasizes the importance of this and of having an available presence who can be authentic and self-aware:

> The opportunity to know oneself, and hence to develop as oneself, requires the availability of a presence which has qualities of receptiveness and responsiveness, based in self-knowledge and in a sense of inner worlds which are honest, not counterfeit. [p. 37]

I have been surprised to encounter a number of social workers who tell me that they no longer like doing their job, and how much they struggle to work with adoptive parents who feel overwhelmed by the challenges of parenting a child with complex needs. As one parent put it: "It's all just too painful, and it doesn't feel as though anything can really change."

It is even harder when these parents are, understandably, frustrated with their social workers for being part of the professional community that had placed the child with them in the first place. This "passing on" of the distress, therefore, can be felt to be more than just a taste of the parents' experience for professionals who are prepared to sensitively challenge and contain these unbearable feelings. They may well find that they are on the receiving end of some surprising reactions.

Melanie Klein, a pioneer in using psychoanalytic methods to treat and understand children, wrote about how the infant remains "within" the older child and adult, and how these infantile experiences and responses to others can help us make sense of the adult's difficulties and preoccupations. She also wrote about how even a child with a fairly healthy relationship with his mother will turn his hatred against the rejecting "denying" or "bad" aspects of the mother's breast (1936), and how the baby "attributes to the breast itself all his own active hatred against it—a process which is termed *projection*" (p. 291).

> One social worker described to me an experience she had found both confusing and upsetting her in her work with an adoptive, parental couple whom she had known for a number of years. The social worker had agreed to meet with the parental couple outside working hours, as finding a time to suit them had proved difficult and she was also fond of them and saw how dedicated they were to their children. However, on this occasion she had been more concerned than usual about how tired and depressed they seemed to be. So she sat with them, hearing and containing their frustrations and feelings of despair and exhaustion, trying to make sense of these feelings. She also arranged to visit the family more regularly and to contact a therapeutic life-story worker who could begin some work with the children and the family as a whole, to gather the painful stories together. Parents said they found the meeting helpful and reassuring and expressed their gratitude. However, when the social worker did not respond promptly to their email the following day, asking a few questions that had arisen after the visit, they became furious and attacking of her. She felt bewildered with their response, treating her as though she had been withholding and neglectful of them and their needs. She was also understandably hurt and disappointed.

This is a familiar scenario for professionals in this line of work, for without being aware of what was going on, this social worker, who had provided a "good feed", suddenly transformed into a withholding, rejecting, "bad" other when she failed to give an immediate response. Her brief absence had provoked primitive feelings of rage and hatred from the infant inside the adult parents, taking everyone by surprise. Such powerful feelings may well have originated in the adoptive children but had then been "projected" into their parents, who had not really known what to do with them but had unconsciously been looking for somewhere to "put" them.

In addition to this very complicated dynamic, there is the tendency to idealize the new person who arrives on the scene with little understanding of all the work that has previously been done with the family. As the new professional "on the block", they will be given all the idealized projections by the struggling parents, leaving the social worker who had done all the hard work of holding the family (potentially for years) feeling rather confused, let down, and rejected themselves.

Donald Winnicott, a psychoanalyst, psychiatrist, and paediatrician, was fascinated by how much the parent–infant relationship can teach us about adults and how they interact with each other. He recognized the huge significance of this primary relationship on the development of the mind and personality of the baby (1945), but he also observed how extreme the baby's feelings could be in response to any change in the mother's availability and her state of mind. These observations of early relationships between mothers and babies helped him to understand the complex dynamics set in motion right at the start of life, which remain influential through into our adult lives in the arena of relationships.

Although Winnicott focused more on what he described as *holding* (1953, 1960) rather than *containment* (Bion, 1962b), he observed something significant about the mother's state of mind in the early weeks after the birth of her baby. He noticed that she showed a more enhanced capacity to connect deeply with her infant and a tendency to become completely preoccupied with the infant—to the exclusion of others (Winnicott, 1953). It was this experience of being central in the mother's mind, according to Winnicott, that enabled the infant to begin life trusting that he would be cared for and held—both emotionally and physically.

Even the hateful or destructive feelings that may have surfaced in the infant in relation to his discomfort can be transformed by the mother in this attentive state, in which she is completely preoccupied with meeting her baby's needs. She is, however, only able to manage and maintain this level of attentiveness for a limited period of time, through being aware of her own feelings, which may at times threaten to overwhelm her. Gradually she will move into being a "good-enough" mother, one who can instinctively find a way of validating her infant's feelings as separate from her own. She will do this by allowing the infant to experience little separations and disappointments, such as having to wait a short while for a feed. Winnicott (1967) described this experience as confirming the infant's very existence: "When I look, I am seen, so I exist" (p. 114).

If, however, a mother is not able to bear the baby's feelings and projections (or separateness) but is only able to see her own version of her baby, then the effect on the infant is markedly different. Alice Miller describes one of Winnicott's images:

> The mother gazes at the baby in her arms, and the baby gazes at his mother's face and finds himself therein . . . provided that the mother is really looking at the unique, small, helpless being and not projecting her own expectations, fears, and plans for the child. In that case, the child would find not himself in his mother's face, but rather the mother's own predicaments. This child would remain without

a mirror, and for the rest of his life would be seeking this mirror in vain. [Miller, 1981, p. 32]

It is this sense of separateness that Winnicott (1953) defined as "me" or "not me", which appears to be far more complicated for an adopted child who may not have had a caretaker attending to or validating the child's feelings and preparing them for separation. I work with many adoptive parents who feel that they are still having to care for the "lost" infant, long after the infant has grown into a child or an adolescent.

One parental couple who adopted three young children told me that they experienced their children as "ever-demanding babies", even though they were now older children, and one of them was approaching adolescence, which meant that they continually struggled to have space for themselves. Unlike the early phase of preoccupation for the mother who has recently given birth, the adoptive parent can quickly start to feel "trapped" or controlled by the intense neediness of his or her child or children. It is as if he or she has entered an enforced state of early (and prolonged) parenthood where there can be no capacity for separate thoughts.

"One day I had no children and the next I had three! But it's like I have three babies who can never be left, even when they need to sleep. They expect me to be there close at hand, and I can feel the life being sucked out of me!"

This is an experience that professionals can relate to, in that one worker described her caseload as being like a large group of siblings, clamouring for attention. Just as things begin to settle for one family in crisis, another would require her urgent and undivided attention, leaving little or no time to recover and prepare for the next crisis.

It is true that some children and young people—and the family as a whole—do need a considerable amount of holding and containing from services over a number of years, although unfortunately this level of support is often not available due to the lack of resources, even though it would save money in the long run. There are, though, some families who seem to continue to access support, even when it may be possible for them to manage more independently. Endings and negotiated separations are important aspects of therapeutic work, but a certain amount of confidence and experience is necessary to ensure that this is prepared for appropriately.

Being aware of transferred feelings or *countertransference* responses can help with this process by facilitating a deeper understanding of the family and making sense of any understandable resistance to change and potential loss. This awareness also facilitates better use of resources and helps professionals to pick out the common threads and emerging patterns from the combined histories within the family as a whole.

Interestingly, where parents are given the space to explore their feelings in a group setting with other parents, they often reflect on how it feels to have children who appear to need far more than they are able to give. They fear that they will never be "good enough", not only for their children but also in the eyes of the professionals supporting them. Feelings of failure and shame are common and can lead to a sense of powerlessness, which can be hard to shift.

When a child transfers his overwhelming feelings onto his parents, who already feel "full up" or exhausted, they can easily get passed down the line or projected onto the professional. If the professional also struggles to *contain* these powerful feelings, then they ricochet around the professional network, creating further splits and difficulties until (hopefully) someone finally gets hold of them.

John Bowlby, a psychoanalyst and psychologist (who had been supervised by Melanie Klein), used his understanding of the relationship or "tie" (1958) between a mother and child to form the basis of what has become widely known as his *attachment theory*. He understood the significance of this connection, but also that of disruptions and separations within this relationship, and how infants express feelings of *protest and despair* in response to their attachment figure (1969). His early ideas about attachment also influenced the work of others, such as Mary Ainsworth (*née* Salter), a developmental psychologist who found a way to formulate Bowlby's theories into methodologies for classifying attachment types (Ainsworth, 1968). She was especially interested in observing and recording a mother's sensitivity to her young child's signals and emotional states, and in the significance for the baby or child of having a parent who is "in tune" with them and able to validate their feelings, survive their rejections, and encourage their authentic communications.

In order to show what this looks like within a therapeutic relationship, I shall draw on some reflections from a clinical session where powerful feelings relating to past rejections and unmanaged separations had surfaced and taken the therapist by surprise.

"The hardest sessions to bear are the ones where the hard won therapeutic relationship can suddenly come apart or feels under attack."

(Child psychotherapy trainee)

For those who work therapeutically with adolescents, there are times when the work is enlivening and exhilarating, but it is rarely comfortable. There are often momentous internal struggles or conflicting desires—to simultaneously connect with others while pushing them away. In this example, the "container", or therapist, had to work extremely hard to take in and then verbalize these contradictory desires for closeness and distance. (The specific details of the session have been anonymized but hold similarities with a number of clinical sessions with adopted young people that I have either delivered or supervised.)

C, a young woman (age 15 years), had been coming for weekly sessions for over six months and had just started to reflect on the losses and shocks in her early life and how they had affected her. She articulated how she was finding it hard to know who she was and what or who mattered most to her. She had also become more aware of how she expressed her fear of rejection by pushing others away. Her psychotherapist used this insight to think about how C used her oppositional behaviour to orchestrate situations where she could express her intense anger and engender feelings of distress in others. C preferred to show anger rather than sadness, which might leave her feeling exposed and vulnerable. She even referred to herself as a "live volcano" that could erupt at any moment. This was especially true if she felt misunderstood or "shown up" in front of others.

Her psychotherapist understood that C's behaviour was a response to her own experiences of loss and abandonment, but she had also come to understand how C would rather sabotage potentially positive relationships than risk intimacy and subsequent loss. C had started to show a greater level of insight, but there were also signs that she was not happy about exposing herself emotionally and becoming more "known" and better understood. She expressed resentment about no longer being able to comfortably evacuate (or project) her painful and unwanted feelings onto others.

There had been some significant struggles over the course of the therapy, including late arrivals and long silences, but C appeared to be beginning to accept the gentle challenge from her psychotherapist, who noted the improved eye contact and an emergence of some friendly banter. This apparent rapport between them led the psychotherapist and C's social worker to assume that C valued her sessions and was getting better. The anger and resentment C had first brought to therapy had also started to dissipate and was replaced by more self-reflection and an insightful perspective on her difficulties and past experiences. She had even started to form ideas about how she wanted to overcome her fears, manage her outbursts, and understand her thought processes.

There were times when it felt to the therapist that she was treading on eggshells, but she was optimistic that she could steer C through this period of emotional turbulence.

However, in what appeared to be a desperate attempt to return to the non-thinking and projecting part of the self, C unpredictably arrived to her session in a furious mood and attempted to "sack" her therapist, screaming accusations at her about how she had neglected and failed her. Her psychotherapist had not anticipated such a rejection or "attack" and found it hard to speak or think. The change had been sudden and shocking, and, as C "stormed out" of the session (early), the therapist was left feeling very concerned that all that she and C had worked on together might have been lost. C vowed never to return, leaving her therapist also feeling bewildered, unwanted, and inadequate. There could be no space for negotiation, there was no warning or apparent triggers, and the therapist felt that she had been on the receiving end of a massive dose of overwhelming feelings.

In supervision, the therapist discussed the confusion and hurt, but also the anger—the *"how could she do this to me?"* feelings, as her incredulity surfaced. Once these feelings had been thought about, though, she was able to think about C's lively and less depressive presentation and how she was bringing more of the "volcano" to the session as well as her adolescent self. On reflection, this provided some hope to the therapist, and she felt able to think and was mindful of the intense emotional pain and bewilderment she had experienced at being accused of failing and causing big losses in C's life. It later transpired that C had felt this fury with her therapist for arriving in her life "too late" and for not having been there for her when she was hurt as a young child.

C had listed numerous others who had been more help to her than her therapist, and although this information was hard to process, it explained just how many lost connections C had experienced in her life, which included professionals. It would appear that C had been preparing herself for her therapist's withdrawal or abandonment, poignantly at the point when she felt most connected to her.

The therapist's feelings were therefore key to understanding C's history of neglect and the destabilizing shock of having lost the little that she did have when she had been removed quite suddenly from her birth mother's care as a toddler. This event had never been fully explained to C, who remembered that even her toys had been left behind when she had been taken into care and that she had been driven away from her home by a social worker she had never met before. The resulting rage had finally found a voice, but the challenge for the therapist was to make sure that this expressed rage did not sabotage the *hard-won* therapeutic alliance.

Allan Schore helpfully expands Bowlby's thoughts about the dual responses to *attachment ruptures* (1994, 2001) of both protest and despair, linking the resulting trauma to a disconnect or mis-attunement between parent and infant. These painful interactions, where the parent cannot act as a mirror and provide containment for the distress, continue to generate further distress in the infant. By refusing to accept the infant's feelings and pushing his or her own distress into the infant, the parent is experienced as unpredictable and potentially harmful, rather than protective. This results in what we have come to understand as a *disorganized attachment* (Schore, 2000), as described by Beatrice Beebe, a clinical professor of medical psychology (in psychiatry), who refers to the infant in this situation as being in a state of "frantic distress" (Beebe, 2006; Beebe & Lachman, 2002).

Over the last decade, researchers in child development have been applying attachment theory to therapeutic work with adults who have experienced relational trauma in childhood, such as Liotti (1992), who links disorganized attachment patterns in infancy with the development of dissociative disorders, as do Allan Schore (1994, 2001, 2003a, 2003b) and Daniel Siegel (1999).

These "push-me, pull-me feelings", as exhibited by C, revealed a more authentic and present state of mind emerging, meaning that she was less likely to dissociate when her conflicting feelings came into contact with each other. However, it did mean that the conflict was very present in the therapeutic relationship and quite a test for C's therapist, who was required to contain and manage it alongside the *frantic distress*. It was a close call, and there had been the very real possibility that C may never have returned to her therapy. There were occasions when the psychotherapist was sorely tempted to "switch off" from C's demands and allow her to leave without offering much resistance. However, with the help of supervision and the consistent support of the social worker, who understood the importance of helping C to stay with the difficult feelings, C was able to return, and the therapeutic relationship was repaired. And despite being somewhat "thrown" by C's explosion and rejection, the therapist persevered with modelling containment and showing sensitivity to C's state of mind during these turbulent times.

There have been other cases where parents or carers (and even other professionals) have taken against the therapist and the therapeutic approach being used. This is especially true when the work becomes challenging or painful and it does not feel possible to wait or contain the anxiety. This situation does need to be guarded against, because it can mean that the avoidance and dissociation is not addressed, resulting in therapy being unsupported or denigrated and therefore ending prematurely.

These kinds of difficulties, rooted in relationships, as already discussed, often require a longer term relationship-based approach in order to earn the trust needed for the therapy to be effective. This can potentially mean keeping a space for a young person despite his or her repeated rejections and missed appointments—a situation that is difficult to justify when resources are stretched. Many services require practitioners to close a case after a number of consecutive missed sessions, meaning that young people with highly challenging behaviours who struggle to engage with services will miss out on much-needed treatment or support.

Children who have experienced intense distress at the hands of their birth parents and have then also been separated from (or abandoned by) them can understandably lack the confidence and internal resources needed to reach out and connect to others in a meaningful or "normal" way. These children and young people also describe how hard they find it to make and keep friends as they struggle to "read" others. One young woman told me that she found that the simple task of trying to make new friends was "exhausting", and every new social situation left her feeling "completely wiped out".

I am aware that I have been drawing from theory to help us to understand very complex processes linked to early relationships between an infant and his or her parents, but I have also highlighted (in chapter 1) how stories can help us to understand these kinds of early separations and relational traumas. The story of Peter Pan is a good example of this, as it illustrates how Peter, an abandoned child, struggles to manage his conflicting feelings when he encounters a "real" mother—Mrs Darling. His fear of this "mother", but also his need for her, puts him in touch with his anger towards his own mother, and he wants to drive Mrs Darling away, preventing her from giving others what he himself has not had.

> Instead of feeling that he was behaving badly he danced with glee. . . .
> He whispered to Tink, "It's Wendy's mother. She is a pretty lady, but not so pretty as my mother. Her mouth is full of thimbles [kisses], but not so full as my mother's was."
> Of course he knew nothing whatever about his mother; but he sometimes bragged about her.
> He did not know the tune, which was 'Home, Sweet Home', but he knew it was saying, 'Come back Wendy'; . . .
> . . . He saw that Mrs Darling had laid her head on the box and that two tears were sitting on her eyes.
> "She wants me to unbar the window," thought Peter, "but I won't, not I." [Barrie, 1863, p. 137]

C had been able to access some liveliness in her therapy, but she had used her challenging behaviour as a way of cutting off or separating from her desire to be held and contained. Once she understood that her challenging behaviour was driven by her sadness and fear of loss, she could acknowledge her yearning for "live company" (Alvarez, 1992), and her more authentic feelings could surface and therefore be addressed.

Establishing a good therapeutic relationship with C required a significant level of resilience and containment, and C's psychotherapist found her supervision to be essential for keeping the work alive and not giving up. She also found it helpful for regulating rather than escalating what Beebe describes as the "frantic distress" (2014) she encountered in C.

Solomon (2018) writes about how difficult it can be for professionals, like social workers, to reflect and offer containment when the work is consistently distressing and demanding:

> There has been a resurgence of an expectation that social workers should build relationships with their clients. Yet what was not articulated and is often still unspoken is how very difficult it is, to be in a relationship with some of the clients that are the bread and butter of a social work caseload. [p. 68]

The overwhelming nature of the work should therefore not be underestimated, for in addition to recognizing "projected feelings", there is a need to understand one's own feelings and personal history and particularly sensitive areas.

Certain themes and corresponding emotions can emerge in adoption work with little or no warning and provoke feelings of disorientation or confusion. Patients have told me about forgetting, on leaving a therapy session, where they had parked their car, but professionals, too, may suddenly start to feel overwhelmed and unable to think—for example, they forget important details about a family's history or, more concretely, find that they have forgotten the name of a parent, child, or young person they have been working with for years.

Adoptive parents I regularly come into contact with talk about the destabilizing effect of caring for children who have suffered disorganized attachments and repeated losses. However, what they say they value most is the consistent, "non-judgmental" company of professionals who are invested in helping them to get hold of their "hard-to-reach" children.

CHAPTER FOUR

What's love got to do with it? Parents in pain

> I want someone who is fierce and will love me until death
> and knows that love is as strong as death, and be on my side
> forever and ever . . .
>
> Jeanette Winterson, *Oranges Are Not the Only Fruit* (1985)

Adoption is an emotive issue, even for those not directly connected to it, but for those who are, such as adoptive parents, emotions can run high. Feelings of failure, shame, and disappointment are common. This chapter is written mainly for adoptive parents and relates specifically to them, acknowledging their dedication to their adopted children and recognizing their struggle. It is also an opportunity for adopters to speak up—to have their say through sharing their own reflections and feelings about their adoptive experience.

Of all the chapters, I think this has been the hardest to write—perhaps because it requires us all to consider the devastating impact adoption can have on parents, their friendships, their couple relationship, their interests and, fundamentally, most of their lives.

I don't think I have ever come across an adopter who expected to have an easy time of it, but I have encountered many who felt that they were unprepared for, or misinformed about, what they would face. Parents who knew that I was writing this book wanted me to make it clear just how difficult it can be for adoptive parents and to emphasize their need for a "life-line" when times are especially hard.

Many adopters have already experienced the loss of not being able to have a biological child, although this is not the case for all. However, as soon as they become adoptive parents, they find that they are having to deal with additional losses, brought into their homes and permeating their lives, by their adopted children, who have had their own difficult histories and significant losses.

Parents have told me how they had once looked forward to a time when they would be free to be a family, to bond with their child or children and get to know them away from the "prying eyes" of social care professionals. But they soon realized that being a family was proving to be far more challenging than they could ever have anticipated. One parent said that he thought this was the main reason why it wasn't possible to manage his adopted children without additional support. He shared that he felt there was a "powerful undercurrent" from the birth family that constantly threatened to pull his children away from him. He hadn't realized just how powerful the birth family influence would be, but he recognized how important it was to find a way to talk about his fear of losing his children to their birth parents. "They [birth parents] are always there somehow in the background, pulling at our children and threatening to sweep them away from us."

Admitting that they are struggling, for some parents, equates to failing, so they "hobble on", as one adopter put it, until they reach a crisis. For others, they may not reach what some might describe as their "breaking point" and feel that things aren't really serious enough to seek help but, nevertheless, experience little enjoyment in their family life, finding that they are becoming more and more exhausted and depressed.

There are, of course, those for whom adoption has worked well without much professional input and who believe that the deep love they have for each other as a family is enough to hold them when things become more challenging. This is rare in my experience, but this may be because families are generally referred to me when they are in crisis. It is, however, important to show balance and reflect how the adoptive process can be positive and that there is such a thing as a good "match", but it is still likely that parents will have plenty of challenges to contend with in addition to the usual demands of family life.

Adoption, for many, can feel like being on a never-ending emotional roller coaster, with times of real exhilaration but also times full of sadness, anxiety, and even terror. Of course, it is to be expected that there will be times for all families when life will be difficult. For adoptive parents and adopted children, the loneliness and isolation is more intense.

These are the families who very much need a community around them and sensitive support from professionals.

I have been helped in the writing of this chapter by honest accounts from parents about their journeys, and it has become increasingly clear to me that it takes a great deal of emotional effort and courage for adopters to ask for help and to share their real story with others. As a professional working in this area, I have learned that taking the time to understand the "real" issues for adoptive parents, even if there are no clear solutions, can help to validate the adopter's experience and counter some of the feelings of isolation, disappointment, and despair.

> "You feel one day like, 'life is ok, we're a family, we can crack this' and then the next it feels as if everything is wrong, maybe even worse than it was before, and no one has the energy to start over. You can feel so alone and you don't want to face anyone. You know that it's never going to be what you hoped for, and that's when you just want to give up . . . you don't feel you're ever going to find your way through it all . . ."

Currently, resources are sorely stretched within mental health services and social care teams, which means that for many families, by the time help arrives, it is perceived to be "too little too late". The lack of resources may also mean that there is a frustrating delay for adopters in getting support. This sets up a complicated dynamic between the professionals and parents, making it very difficult for them to establish a trusting alliance. In turn, this lack of trust then leads to an anticipation of rejection or an expectation of failure. The tension between the state who provided the child for the parents and the parents who provided a home for the child can be difficult to resolve.

Rejection and loss permeates families and professional networks, sometimes in subtle ways, such as through unforeseen staff changes, when a social worker changes roles or goes on long-term sick leave; but there are times when a "case" will be mysteriously reallocated or even closed. There may also be complaints that rumble away behind the scenes, indicating that a bigger storm is on its way. Beleaguered professionals feel scrutinized and criticized by adoptive parents who may well have felt judged and scrutinized themselves. Things can then start to go wrong, meaning that "errors" are more likely to occur, but these are also more difficult to admit to or reflect on, and so the cycle of distrust and neglect continues.

Parents have told me that when they try to challenge issues, they can feel as if they are being seen as uncooperative or "confrontational", whereas professionals report that some adoptive parents show little understanding of the pressure they are under and the lack of support they themselves are struggling with. This complex situation only exacerbates the feelings of powerlessness and distress and causes some parents and professionals to withdraw from each other or give up their protest altogether. Other parents may increase their protestations and wage a "war" on local authorities. This simply replicates patterns of conflict and fury with professionals, features of the child's history within his birth family. Some parents also admit to feeling that they have lost themselves and have become stuck in a place of conflict where they are proliferating distress. However, the statement that comes up repeatedly is: "We didn't sign up to this."

For any adopted young people reading this, it may sound as though adoptive parents have huge regrets about adopting. This is really not the case, but painful feelings and difficulties will arise from bringing together people whose lives have already been affected by trauma, separation, and loss. Without the right support, it can be hard to know how to transform these feelings and experiences into something meaningful for the whole family.

These challenges for adoptive families are becoming more publicly known and spoken about in the media, but they are no less painful. What is more, the divisions and rifts between young people and their parents, or between parents and professionals, can last for a very long time, making it hard for the wounds to be tended to or to have the chance to heal. Some parents are still trying to claim their children after years of difficulty and what they perceive to be continuous rejections. One mother described her sense of shame in acknowledging her problems in bonding with her adopted son as a baby. She confessed that she had not allowed professionals to get close to her for fear that they would see that she didn't, or couldn't, love him.

> "I've never quite got the measure of him. He didn't feel or smell right to me, it was so hard, and it's still hard. I had thought about asking if he could go back—but I didn't know how I could do that, so I just got on with it in the end, but it's as if we still just keep missing each other . . ."

To parents who have been unable to have birth children, this rupture, this not managing to come together, can feel like a reminder of previous lost or "missed" conceptions. This re-evokes painful memories of past failures to create life, feelings of impotence, and a sense of being painfully different from others.

Winnicott said: "There is no such thing as an infant"—there is a baby and someone (1960, p. 39fn.). But the challenges are huge when taking on children with complex histories and becoming an important "someone" for the adopted child.

Adopted children and young people are also facing their own enormous challenges, like quickly having to become acclimatized to a new family and building attachments in totally alien environments. The shock and destabilizing effect of this experience on children's personalities, especially after numerous losses, can be difficult to quantify. What enables families to stay together through all of this remains a mystery to me, but the role of professionals in providing support during the darkest times is crucial. The value of sticking it out and being willing to be alongside families for a big chunk of their journey must not be underestimated.

The writing of this book has allowed me to learn more about different adoption journeys and how so many parents, even those who are struggling, are still invested in being a family but, however, cannot do it alone. They genuinely appreciate professionals who have grown to understand them over time, but they naturally feel frustrated with those who seem to want to make swift judgements, or who will only offer short-term advice and formulations—never really getting hold of the family or fully grasping the complexity or the level of risk.

There are many services that have emerged since the inception of the Adoption Support Fund, but these are not designed to work with universal services collaboratively, nor do they usually deliver ongoing and accessible treatment or support throughout the adoption journey. Unfortunately, this means that many of the parents I see feel that they have had repeated assessments, but there is no one who will work with them and their children for the longer journey. They are left facing a greater awareness of the difficulties and sometimes, therefore, coping with more emotional pain about the severity of the problems, but with no additional support. I have been told politely by parents and social workers that those who undertake these assessments can be like "well-resourced foster carers" who can give notice on the children in their care at any point and have the luxury of referring on to other professionals if things get tough or if they don't know what to do next.

One parent explained how an assessment that had furnished her with a helpful diagnosis for her child did not then lead on to the provision of ongoing support as she had expected. She tried to articulate what it feels like to be told by an "expert" that your child has significant or complex needs and then not to be given the resources to meet those needs.

"These so called experts don't have to endure the devastation of being at the centre of our painful story. They hold their bit of my child, but it's such a little piece really."

Parents repeatedly tell me that they will cling on to anything they are offered in a desperate search for a solution or for a better understanding about why their child is experiencing difficulties. Having a clear explanation or diagnosis can help to alleviate the underlying distress of not knowing what to do and feeling powerless about their situation. Any hopes they have about "fixing" things, however, mostly lead to disappointment and more frustration.

Good assessments are necessary for a number of reasons, such as picking up neurological difficulties and disorders where medication or a specific treatment or approach is indicated, or to gather information that can be useful for the family and all those who support the family. However, what is less useful is identifying difficulties that require significant resources that may not then be available within local services. One parent of an adopted and learning-disabled child voiced her concern that professionals she had worked with only seemed interested in hearing about their story rather than having a significant role within it.

"It's as if no one wants to stay with us. Everyone is looking for a reason to pass us (or my son) on to someone else."

This apparent lack of interest, or of a longer term investment in adoptive families with complex issues, is not personal. It can be linked specifically to the way in which services are designed and commissioned. This situation also highlights the gaps of provision in some services, where children and young people with complex difficulties and disorders do not seem to meet the threshold or fit the referral criteria to get the treatment they need. Most public sector services are (at the time of writing) under huge pressure to heavily filter referrals, signpost on to other services, or only offer a limited number of sessions.

There are parents who feel "exonerated" when their child has been given a mental health diagnosis, as it helps them to have a way of explaining why their child behaves or presents differently from others. It is sad that adoptive parents feel that they need to have a label in order to feel more "accepted" or to receive sympathy from others. It is not surprising, then, that some parents withdraw from social situations and start to give their apologies for not attending extended family gatherings.

When the situation for the family becomes intolerable, there is, of course, a risk of placement breakdown or disruption. One of the most likely times for this to happen is when an adopted child or young person becomes an adolescent. During this time, the fear of loss and response to separation is intense, but it can also feel like the birth family has suddenly "rocked up" (as one adopter put it) in the adoptive family. The difference between the adopted child and her parents can also become more accentuated at this time, and both the young person and the parent(s) can struggle to accept each other or find a way to "fit" together.

I spoke to one adoptive mother who explained that she wouldn't have chosen this particular child, had she known what he would be like as a young adult. She had tried to teach her son her own values, coming from a strict upbringing herself. She spoke about her disappointment at not being able to influence her son's behaviours, life choices, and sense of identity in the way she had hoped. She related this to the creative process of knitting or sewing and how, if you follow a pattern closely, you can reassuringly create your version of the pattern with your own subtle touches.

> "You have a clear understanding of what the finished project would look and feel like."

She had thought that there might have been similarities with the adoption process and had not been prepared for the shock of discovering how different her son was—physically and emotionally—from herself, or how much he would grow to resemble his birth family. I have also heard other adopters use the knitting analogy. Perhaps alongside the mystery of growing a unique human being is the surprise of not being able to predict how things will turn out, despite putting so much of oneself into a "growing" child. This can, of course, also be true of birth children, but it is likely to be more complicated for an adopted child and his or her adoptive parents.

> "I wouldn't have knitted him this way if I'd had a choice, I would have opted for a different pattern."
>
> *(Parent)*

I am reminded here of the biblical quote:

> For you created my inmost being; you knit me together in my mother's womb. I praise you because I am fearfully and wonder-fully made. [Psalm 139, *New International Version*]

This is a different take on how so much of the individual's identity has already been formed before birth, as I have previously touched on, and how helping an individual grow up to be uniquely him/herself is a huge responsibility and a challenge as well as a privilege.

Perhaps it is harder to reflect on the wonder and mystery of the making and "growing" of a human being when adopters are repeatedly reminded that they have not physically "made" their child and that the child does not have their genetic imprint. This can, unfortunately, lead to an assumption that their adopted children are very different from them, not only biologically but also in how they feel and express themselves. There is no evidence to suggest that this is the case, but the surprise at what their adopted children become in adolescence can mean that their children feel doubly alien to them. This awareness of difference can shake the young person's and the parents' sense of their young person as being connected to them. It can also send shock waves through their long-established family foundations and significant relationships. This is where creating opportunities to have these honest conversations can be incredibly important for families (parents and children or young people) who feel they have to hide their resentment and disappointment.

Sometimes providing respite for a family going through a crisis around identity can allow for more of a thinking space for the past and painful losses to be processed in a different way. Potentially destabilizing feelings can then begin to find a voice, away from the stressful home situation, and allow new thoughts and ideas to emerge about what it means to be a family.

I spoke to Jane Drew, a post-adoption support social worker, who has worked with me in our local specialist adoption service (AdCAMHS) and who has helped a number of families over the years to survive potential placement disruptions. I wondered what it was that specifically helped to bring about a meaningful change for these families. She explained that there are times when members of a family simply need a break from each other as they cannot get out of what has become a destructive pattern or cycle. As a senior practitioner, she has provided continued commitment to adoptive families, including those in crisis, and, in some cases, she has maintained contact with birth parents as well as adopters and their children right through from placement to young adulthood.

I asked her about what mattered most with regard to supporting parents to "keep hold of" their children who appear to be very different from themselves. She tells me that what she has learned through her work with adoptive families over the years, is the centrality and significance of good relationships:

"Good practice in social work has historically been about establishing meaningful relationships with families in need. I see no reason why this should change. Despite the challenge we face in our work, families are more likely to accept the difficult decisions we make as social workers if we have established an appropriate and secure relationship with them. This is what engenders a deeper understanding of the problems and grows a healthy respect for each other. It also means that when children become adolescents, they already know us and can tell us what they need. They are also more able to let us know what is really going on at home."

Bower and Solomon (2018) write about the challenge for social workers of building meaningful and trusting relationships with families, even from the first encounter:

It is common to do a home visit feeling quite alright and come out feeling disheartened, confused or guilty. [p. 9]

I wondered with Drew why so many families seem to have to reach a crisis point before they can access the support they need.

"Resources need to focus more on building good relationships through supporting social workers to get to know their families by providing the right forums for them to think about their work. Too often, social workers will refer a case on for treatment without ever having met the child or young person, because the work, even after the first visit, stirs up so much within themselves."

She added that being listened to and understood makes such a difference in this respect, after the initial shock or surprise of meeting a family who need to "unburden" themselves. Drew thinks this kind of listening or "soaking up" by the social worker is especially vital for adoptive children and their families who feel that they have lost their voices or that no one wants to hear what they have to say.

"They need to be given opportunities to use their voices, when in the past they have been silenced or their distress ignored."

After some reflection, Drew expressed some emotion about the privilege of being a social worker and being invited into people's homes and their most private worlds and feelings. She talked about the adolescents she has kept in touch with and how rewarding it has been to work with them.

"Although it can be tiring, it's also a great joy to work with young people who contact you when they need help and who want to share their thoughts and feelings with you. I have been called by young people who have run away, and no one else knows where they are. They want to find a way back home, but they often feel ashamed and lonely, and they have no idea how to sort things out. I have seen young people at breaking point where they can tell me honestly that they can't go on, they don't want to leave home but they also just can't stay. I have also witnessed some painful confrontations between young people and their parents, and I can see that they are desperate to connect with each other, but they keep getting 'stuck'.

Making it possible for them to find each other again and move out of a stuck place is worth every bit of effort. That's the part of the work I enjoy most."

We reflected on young people and parents we had worked with together and those who had needed to stay with family friends or spend some time in respite care, in order to allow us to do some separate work with them and their parents. This had helped them to reconnect as a family—an approach that had been especially helpful for adolescents who had started to express their rage and distress more forcefully, and who found it very difficult to allow others to get close to them.

One young person developed a strategy with us for managing destructive and highly anxious adolescents. A quote from her, which other parents have found particularly helpful, explains the communication behind the "push-me, pull-me" behaviours:

"They may be pushing you away, but they also want you to stay. It doesn't work, though, if you get right into a young person's face when they are kicking off. The message they are really giving you is: 'Get out of my face, but not out of my life'."

Together we thought about an approach to getting alongside the young person, explaining where the parents will be when the young person is ready to find them, but, very importantly, to continue to allow them their emotional space. Once they do approach, she suggested slowly walking and encouraging the young person to join them. He or she can then follow at his or her own pace, until ready to come alongside the parent. Even then, conversation is not always possible, but young people do need to know that big feelings can be tolerated until they can be talked about comfortably. This is very different from condoning destructive, controlling, or aggressive behaviours, but it avoids the risk of tackling things head on in the heat of the moment.

This young person, now an adult who works with young people herself, has kindly given her permission for me to share her reflections. She also wants parents to understand that when they push hard to be loved and accepted or want desperately to "fix" the problem, it feels "too hot" for young people who have relational difficulties. Knowing when to "back off a bit" without "sulking" is vital if parents are going to survive this phase—which, unfortunately, can go on for years!

Drew agreed with this but added:

> "Young people do need to feel accepted, however hard that is. For me, they maintain the capacity to make me smile, even when they are challenging. Seeing the little child inside the adolescent helps, as does humour, which can be an essential ingredient for regulating frustrations without glossing over the pain or the struggles."

Providing opportunities for adopted young people and their parents to have more of a political or public voice is one way of addressing the powerlessness and is something we have done within AdCAMHS. Adopted young people were delighted when they were given the opportunity to visit the Children's Commissioner and the Minister of State for Children and Families, saying that it helped to validate their experiences and gave them a new confidence. If listened to and taken seriously, they will communicate openly about their experiences and views. We, as professionals and policymakers, have a great deal to learn from these young people and their experiences.

I interviewed a parental couple who feel strongly that politicians should be told about the important issues relating to adoption and how much parents are "holding" for the state. As a parental couple, they had made a choice to adopt fairly early into the process of wanting children. They have two adopted children who have complex birth family histories, which included parental violence, substance misuse, and mental health difficulties. Even as babies, these children had already been negatively affected by their birth families.

It is unlikely that all of these issues and challenges were going to be completely resolved, but this couple were able to reflect on what they valued the most about being supported by a specialist adoption service. One positive they highlighted was the "long-haul commitment" they received and having the same social worker for years, working alongside psychotherapists, to think about the specific mental health needs of their children. This, they felt, had been the most appropriate support package for their family and had enabled them to feel understood and "held", despite the ongoing challenges they faced as a family and as a parental couple.

> "It's like we share a history—our history is yours too, you as professionals share in the parenting of our children in some ways, because you hold us

and then we feel more able to hold our children, even when it is very hard to keep hold of them. You have therefore provided us with an extended professional family over the years, and there is nothing to match that. All the difficult stuff can be shared, which leads to a greater feeling of trust between us. This trust then gets passed down to our kids, and we can find our way round some very tricky situations. We feel that there's nothing that can't be said or thought about—which somehow makes us all feel safer. It also helps to know that we have somewhere to go where we can be authentic."

I asked about what it was that enabled them to take hold of the positive experiences of being supported, as I was aware that I had encountered other parents who had been disparaging about receiving support from a public sector-funded service.

"There are times when one of us will remember something that one of you has said to us, and it really helps. It can feel irritating, for example, to have your partner quote it back to you, like, 'match the intensity' and then I want to say to you, 'it's easy for you, you don't have to live with this situation the way we do 24/7'. But then, when we think it through, it does make sense and it's like you're with us somehow, still helping us in the background."

I reflected on the feelings of exhaustion and disappointment that adopters talk about, which can lead to feelings of anger and resentment, the feelings that so often get redirected to others.

"If as an adopter of complex children, you can let go of the anger about the fact that you are dealing with this stuff every day, then you can start to listen to what is really being said, and it can make a difference. We feel more able to manage our expectations and disappointments these days, but part of that is that we know that we have somewhere to go with these difficult feelings."

(Father)

"As a couple we have been prepared to reach out and ask for help when we've needed it. We've also been fortunate that our reaching out has been responded to, but we haven't put a barrier up for professionals the way that I know some adopters do. It is important to trust the process: you don't get anywhere by continually needing others to know how angry and upset you are. We don't know if that's about us or our situation, we haven't had anywhere else to go, so we have to make use of what's there for us. We don't have a family around us, for instance. Our children are our family. We both feel strongly that it's not about blood; you as professionals are part of our family and our children know you and trust you. They also know we speak to you and that we all think about them, together."

(Mother)

I asked them what it was that they felt adopters or prospective adopters needed to know:

"The most important thing for all parents to understand, and we have been on our own journey with this, is that throwing money at a problem generally doesn't resolve it. There is a prevailing feeling in our culture that if you spend enough money, the difficulty will dissipate. This isn't true; we spend time with our children, getting to understand their nature, which may be different from ours, but our relationship with them comes first. We both work, but we value our children and our relationship to them over and above earning money. The first thing we do when there is problem is take time to understand it with them—and it does take time."

They felt that this approach was relevant for professionals and politicians too—providing the right resources or a good support service

"is not about the glossy brochure or good marketing. What's most important is to support authentic relationships. People who don't value relationships maybe haven't experienced good relationships themselves."

They also talked about how relationships can be messy, but that the best ones are built on a long-standing commitment. "We have the sense that 'you're in it with us'."

I asked about love and how "easy" it is to talk about love, but what does this really mean to a parent when your children can be hard to love or may not want to receive your love?

"In adoption you make a family in whatever way works. It's important to embrace your children and really welcome them into your family, even if this means learning to let go sometimes. I can honestly say that our love increases for our children, and I realize that they are amazing! We have also found that there are echoes of our own life experiences as we learn more about our children and their birth histories. We are different, and yet we are similar and going through this together. That difference doesn't divide us."

They also added that they felt that the main ingredients for building a strong family were:

"Love, determination, clear communication, ongoing commitment, and creating a shared family story which everyone can accept."

They have found a way to "smile" in the face of difficulty and trauma that is not disingenuous, but shows their care and affection for each other and their desire for honesty. This helps to soften the blow and enables them to absorb the impact of the trauma together. This brings to mind a limerick by Edward Lear from 1846 :

There was an Old Man who said, "How
Shall I flee from this horrible cow?
I will sit on this stile,
And continue to smile,
Which may soften the heart of that cow."

Learning to understand and accept each other's stories is an important process for adoptive families, as explored in chapter 1, but these stories may turn out to be more shocking than parents had first anticipated. Drew emphasized the need to work with parents and to give them a platform to speak about their experiences more publicly.

"Some parents have lost their way or have not been safe carers for the children placed in their care, but these are really the minority. Most adoptive parents have dedicated so much of their lives and have gone to hell and back to support their children. We need to work with them rather than antagonize them if we are to keep families together."

The parents I interviewed felt that coming to terms with their children's real-life stories has allowed for a greater acceptance of their children and their complex difficulties.

"There's a murder in our family story; we have taken that story into our hearts with our children because their story has now become our story. It's like we inhabit each other's stories and we're all in this chapter, together."

Another way of bringing together different kinds of adoption stories can be to create forums and environments where adoptive parents can share their experiences with each other. In our adoption service, we do this through therapeutic parenting groups. These groups are different from groups for parents that focus mainly on parenting techniques and strategies. We aim to help parents build more secure and trusting relationships with their children and with each other as parents. These relationships develop over the course of the group as adopters learn about each other's journey.

Towards the end of the group, a poem is written collectively by parents as part of a therapeutic group process; it covers feelings and statements from each of the parents, but it is put together by the group as a whole to describe their collective experience. It can be a genuine moment of awareness and a point of emotional connection for the members of the group. I am fortunate to have permission to share one of these poems, which describes the different perspectives and contradictions adoptive parents feel about caring for their children and what it means to them to be a parent. It is a very different way of bearing witness to the determination of adoptive parents to stand by their children or, as one parent put it, "to keep trying to reach out to and get hold of my children." Our thanks to the TPG parents who have allowed this poem to be shared.

Group poem—Our journey as adoptive parents

Feeling and being different—But we're so tired
On this emotional roller coaster ride
Joy and hope was where we started
With a belief in our ability to be good
"Make a difference" parents
We will heal, help. And our love . . .
Will conquer all
But this love we have
Is a painful kind of love
We love you beyond belief—but God it is hard
You, child—completed us
We became a family—what we all longed for
A better life—and more together
We would still do it—all over
And our lives are richer—but "ouch"
This is not how we planned it
Parenthood is tougher than we expected it to be
It's an uphill challenge but we're always learning . . .
How enormous this love is
It seeps through the cracks and tests our bond
We cling to each other
And we achieve so much—together
The energy, the character
Crazy can be good
What we all need—to feel alive
It was all worth it
But—also "what have we done?"

There is no way back
Here we are together
Deep feelings
And with these different eyes
We now see:
Such truths and absurdity, but spirit
And stories that make us laugh out loud
So learn from us and let us teach you
About the beauty, wonder, pain
And aliveness
Of our world, our child—our family.

CHAPTER FIVE

A different kind of normal: the voices of young people

Most of the time I feel lost, like I'm living the wrong life . . .

Young person, age 17 years

When I think of the adopted young people I have worked with over the years, I can recall a number of conversations about the challenge of negotiating the hazardous and tumultuous time of being an adolescent. It is a time when new ideas and questions about identity and belonging will emerge, often triggering a deeper awareness of losses and insecurities from the past.

In addition to these issues is a phenomenon that I have come to describe as the "call of the wild" for adopted young people, who may experience the "draw" of their birth family like they have never experienced it before. I shall refer to this in more detail later on, but what seems to be happening for adopted adolescents, with new drives and desires, is that they start to feel more connected to the adults who conceived them: their birth parents.

Most adopted children and young people, when given the opportunity, will talk about feeling conflicted or "divided" during their adolescence. Although this goes with the territory in this time of transition, it is more complicated for adopted young people. It can feel to them as if every significant decision they makes will align them with either "one side or the other"—or, as one young person described it, pleasing either his birth family or his adoptive parents. For example, they may have adoptive parents for whom succeeding at school and getting good grades is important, while their birth parents left school with few qualifications or aspirations. This can potentially create a conflict, and the pull of these two different paths and very different models for becoming an adult can lead to confusion and paralysis. For a young person who is struggling to work out what he or she is good at or wants to be, "success" is a confusing concept and may be associated with the hopes and expectations of his or her adoptive parents, whereas so-called failure is attributed to the birth parents. It is therefore very hard for an adopted young person to genuinely find his or her own path and manage his or her internal conflicts.

In Philip Pullman's *Northern Lights (His Dark Materials)* trilogy (published between 1995 and 2000), the main character, Lyra, who is adopted by a *"gyptian"* family, struggles to find her sense of identity and to work out where she truly belongs. In the world she inhabits, all the humans have animal souls or *daemons*, who represent a part of the self. These daemons take the form of creatures and are a different gender from the human they belong to/with. In children, these so-called daemons are shape-shifters and frequently transform in order to communicate something about the personality, emotions, and state of mind of their human. They also have a name and provide companionship as well as offering the capacity to reflect. In this respect, each child can learn about his or her true self, as defined by Winnicott (1960), through interacting with his or her daemon. Once the child has matured into a young adult, the shape "settles", and the core self is static. As coming-of-age books, the trilogy examines the journey from childhood to adolescence, identifying what children take from their parents and their environment but also what young adults will need in order to "settle" and find their unique and separate selves.

In the first book of the trilogy there are so-called *scientific experiments* carried out on children to see what happens when the daemon is severed from the rest of the personality. What becomes painfully apparent is that cutting away the core and emotional aspects of the child, including their experiences (good and bad), only leaves them feeling incomplete and bereft. The child then begins psychologically to "waste away".

Lyra asks her daemon why some adults choose to hurt children:

"Why do they do these things to children, Pan? Do they all hate children so much, that they want to tear them apart like this? Why do they do it?" [p. 389]

Many adopted children ask this question in connection with the childhood abuse or neglect they have suffered, but also with their experience of being "severed" from their birth parents/family and a core part of themselves. Some children do feel as if they have been part of a cruel experiment where their "best-known" selves became lost or were removed from them.

I describe in chapter 3 how when children are separated from their birth parents there is a fundamental and potentially life-changing loss to absorb (even if the birth parents were abusive) and how they may respond to such a sudden separation by closing down or pushing others away. This does not mean that babies or children should be left to suffer, but it is important to recognize that they are unlikely to feel grateful or pleased about such a loss. One way that adolescents respond to this loss is to use their new but fragile independence to run. The running can happen in a number of ways, but it appears to be motivated by the need to escape from powerful feelings that have only become stronger in adolescence.

> There are few situations in life which are more difficult to cope with than an adolescent son or daughter during the attempt to liberate themselves. [Anna Freud, 1958, p. 278]

I have come across a number of adopted young people who "run". They may be running away from their adoptive home or are trying to find their birth family. Sometimes the running is simply a way of communicating distress. Running away presents new and increased risks, which parents and professionals find difficult to deal with. Even those young people who seem relatively "settled" in their adolescence speak about times when they need to run away. It is difficult to explain why this is; perhaps it relates to the experience of adoption and how, as young children, they learned that the only thing to do when things get really tough is to quickly remove oneself from the situation.

I have tried to explore this with young people by making the distinction between being removed in order to become safe, as opposed to running away from relative safety in response to overwhelming feelings. I have also reflected on how the running can take young people into alien and unsafe environments, where they risk losing more than the freedom to make their own decisions. Adopted young people have had at least one experience of being thrust into an alien environment, so it may be that running away holds a certain attraction and familiarity for them or that something is being re-enacted through the act of running.

What continues to intrigue me is the manner in which many children and young people take flight, such as running off without their shoes. This barefoot "flight" is reminiscent of familiar fairy tales, like the Grimms' *Hansel and Gretel*, where the children suddenly learn that they are in danger and hastily escape. In the Grimms' earlier version of the tale, the woodcutter's wife, who wants to have the children killed, is the children's biological mother, and the father (the wood-cutter) colludes with her plan. In later revised editions, the wife is the children's stepmother, and the woodcutter is, supposedly, unaware of her scheme. The children, however, are not killed: they are abandoned and left to their own devices but are helped by the natural world around them, a world that feels less threatening to the children than their home.

The fairy tale may have originated in the medieval period of the Great Famine in Europe (1315–1321), when parents were forced to abandon their children in the woods when they could no longer feed them. In both versions of the tale, the abandoned children come across a witch deep in the wood who wants to cook them and eat them. The phrase "out of the frying pan and into the fire" comes to mind, and, unfortunately, for some adopted children, their "new" family may also turn out to be unsafe or abusive. This is rare, but it does happen, which is a tragedy and travesty for children who have been betrayed twice by the adults who were meant to protect them.

The children in the fairy tale do, however, manage to outwit the witch (who falls into the fire herself) and then finally find their way home. The fact that the stepmother dies at the exact point that the witch falls into the fire indicates that she and the witch are connected or are the same, but also that the children are only able to return home once the unsafe parent has gone.

Perhaps the gradual remembering of the birth family or the "call of the wild" for the adopted young person introduces a new but potentially dangerous area of conflict into the adoptive home. As in the tale of Hansel and Gretel, the home that had once felt safe suddenly feels threatening and causes the children to flee without taking anything with them, not even their shoes!

> "We [adopted young people] have all been let down by people and we've all felt really alone—but some of us have had so much s**t that it's hard to know who to go to when things are messed up . . . you just have to get out and sort it yourself."
>
> *(Young person—age 17 years)*

One young person who was adopted at the age of 5 years described how painful but also complicated her adoption had been, moving from her neglectful birth family to foster carers, who later became her adopters.

"There were times when it felt worse than being with my birth parents: at least I knew them and how to escape from them. But my new parents . . . well, they tried to be nice, and I didn't want to hurt them or ruin it all, but I couldn't really be myself. I was used to mess and helping myself to food if it was there; I could fend for myself. Then all of a sudden, I had to like . . . try to speak to people about my day and stuff, and there were all these rules. I was so scared—I didn't know what was going on—I couldn't escape. All I kept thinking about was my dog and my stuff and being back at home. I just wanted to run away . . ."

(Young person, age 15 years)

I interviewed a young person, L, with her parents' permission, who very much wanted to speak about her desire to run and to keep on running. I think she also wanted to be interviewed because it was her way of explaining to her adoptive parents and to other adopters why this happens. She is still receiving therapy from a child psychotherapist and has considerable support from the professional network around her, but her early experiences of loss and trauma are central to her difficulties and became the main focus for the interview.

I felt that L also used the interview to say "sorry" to her parents for running away, and she wanted to acknowledge that she knew her parents genuinely loved her. She said that she runs because she wants to find her way back to her birth mother and continues to feel like a "lost" baby who wants and needs her "mummy".

At other times she thinks she runs to escape from home because "they [her adoptive parents] get in my face", and there are those times when she deliberately runs into the path of danger, unable to resist the "call of the wild"—a phrase she could relate to.

"It's hard to show emotion about your birth parents to your adoptive parents—when you do care about them but not in the same way. You kind of know you don't really belong with them [adoptive parents]. You spend your life not really knowing who you are and where you belong, but there is this yearning. People don't get what that's like . . ."

I asked her why she felt that her birth family had such power over her, despite having had very little contact with them since birth.

"My early life started off hard—I was born addicted, and my birth mum just left. I hate her, and I don't want to love her, she abandoned me—but somehow, I do, I kind of want to be like her, to be close to her. It's in me . . . I can't explain it. Your birth family is really important even if you don't want them to be. You can't help it. It's like, I *was* upset when

I heard that my birth dad had died, but I didn't want to show it. I didn't want to hurt my adoptive parents. So my feelings were fake—but I didn't know what else to do."

I asked L to describe her feelings about her birth mother leaving so soon after she was born.

"It's unfair, I feel disgusted, alone. . . . I know that since that day, I'm not right inside. I keep wanting to go back there. I just keep going back . . ."

In terms of how this has affected her current relationships and her capacity to connect with others, she said:

"I get attached really easily to people, but then I push them away. I have been hurt and I have hurt others so many times, but it all goes back to that first hurt . . .

My adoptive parents . . . they are good to me, and I am grateful to them . . . I admire them, but I can't stop being hurt and angry about what happened. My birth mum, I don't really know her, but I'm curious about her and why she was who she was . . . what happened to her? It must be heart-breaking for my parents bringing up a kid who's not theirs and them seeing me turning out how I am."

When I commented on the power that L's birth mother seemed to have over her, she agreed.

"My love for my birth mum is toxic—it's powerful. She tried to kill herself after I was born . . . she didn't deserve to have us kids, but it's difficult having two families, two lives. It would be more truthful to admit that, but I find it hard to be honest. This other life, this other self is always there. More so now. . . . You feel split in two. Always split and there's no way to bring it all together in my mind."

I wondered why L felt that there was no way to bring the two lives or selves together. L considered that this might be possible, but that she would need to find a way to be "at home" in herself first.

"I guess you have to find your own way to be at home. You need to explore and find what works. You know what fits. I used to have imaginary friends, they were like parts of me—different parts of me that helped to hold me together. I still talk to them sometimes. I gave them names. One of them was more like my birth family. She's still in there, but mostly they just help me to find the "middle me". I've got to find my own path—that's what I'm trying to do. My imaginary friends helped me to do that when I was younger."

L was able to reflect on how hard it is for her to think, to remember the path she should be taking. It is especially hard when she thinks about her birth mother and how this loss permeates (my word, not hers) her life. One of the ways she deals with this is to use substances.

> "My thoughts are hard to control now. I have to block them out. I want my mum—my mummy—my birth mummy. That baby wants her mummy. It never goes away, I am that baby, I kind of know somewhere inside me what I should do to take care of myself, of her. But when I'm high or drunk, it's like being back in the womb, it's like you believe you can start over. Noises and feelings are muffled or distant, and I don't feel the pain. It's a place where you can believe you can start over. It might all be ok. That's why I'm hiding in that place now. I'm like that baby wanting her mummy. I like the escape—like when I'm drinking, although I'm scared I'll end up more like my Dad, who was an alcoholic. I want to rewrite my life . . . from the beginning."

We both acknowledged that a "rewriting" would require a great deal of courage and support, and L admitted that she wasn't really ready to do this. I asked her about her reasons for running and the challenge of keeping her safe. What she would say to other young people who are on the run and can't find their way home?

> "Don't give up. There are days when you will struggle and you'll have times when you will run and hide—but you need to remember that it can and will get better. But only if you really want it to! The storms keep coming, but it's important to hold on to those who love you. Try not to be ashamed of being broken and having a broken life . . . and family isn't always blood. I've done things I'm not proud of and others judge me because of what I do to get by. But deep down, I do know what the right path is . . ."

L has needed considerable support from the professional network around her, including the provision of a more secure setting in order to limit the damage she could do to herself through running. This is a huge challenge in terms of resources for services managing these kinds of difficulties, but also for adopters, who are likely to be unaware of the level of complexity their baby or young child brings with them to their family.

A further complication or difficulty for young people like L is their ability to find unsafe people, or to "find" the birth family without adoptive parents or professionals knowing. In these times of ever-developing technological advances, there are additional risks arising through the way that we humans choose to communicate with each other. Personal information and contact details are more easily accessible (through social

media) than ever before. This means that there are additional tempta-
tions as well as risks that are hard for young people and their parents
to regulate. Young people have told me how they were able to locate a
birth family member with as little as a name and a vague idea of what
they might look like.

Helping teenagers manage themselves in different forums and having unplanned contact with their birth family is therefore more challenging than it used to be. Not so long ago, letterbox contact was the
main channel for communication between adopted children and their
birth families, a contact that was mediated by professionals and parents.

Now, social media sites, such as Facebook, Twitter, and Instagram,
have dramatically affected the way that adopted children or birth families can make contact with each other. These sites have also made it much
easier to bypass the usual safeguarding processes put in place to ensure
that contact with birth families is safe and reasonable.

The additional pressure from social media to "fit in" can also cause
difficulty, and there may be little respite from this, even at home. These
challenges and dilemmas were originally covered in a guide for Community Care Inform written in 2010 by Eileen Fursland, which was later
updated by Julia Feast and Elaine Dibben (2017).

Some of these themes and others relating to the way adopted young
people deal with the challenges of the modern world and their sense of
identity can be addressed in a group setting. Every year, I and a social
work colleague run a group for adopted young people between the ages
of 13 and 17 years. We have been astounded by how much young people
learn from each other in these groups—and what we can learn from them.

The group follows a 12-week programme and culminates in a woodland camp. It covers topics such as how to connect safely with others,
self-awareness, and identity, and it explores more personal issues relating to change and loss. There are usually around ten young people in
the group, which is held in a community arts centre and is therefore
more accessible for young people than a CAMHS clinic. It is facilitated
by two therapists and two to three social workers, and the curriculum
and programme are adapted each year to "fit" the specific needs of the
referred young people. It follows an attachment-theory-based model,
with the opportunity for channelling any potential "acting out" within
a stage area. The stage itself provides the opportunity to use drama to
act out and make sense of experiences, feelings, and behaviours and to
find a more confident and public voice to express them.

A great deal of thought goes into preparing for the group, as many
of the referred young people already struggle with group situations.
This environment will pose a new challenge for them and for us, and
there are always risks attached to bringing a group of vulnerable young

people together under one roof. Having a clear plan and programme, shared with other professionals, helps to alleviate some of the anxiety about getting started, but it also provides additional safety while allowing space for creative expression.

This desire to plan in readiness for "new arrivals" is an important part of preparing one's mind for the potential challenges of group work and could relate to the beginning of an adoptive journey—which (in most cases) starts with a plan. Plans vary, but parents and the placing social worker usually aim to draw up an acceptable version in order to address the challenges and demands of the first weeks and months of welcoming a new child into a family. The plan should include information about support available beyond the adoption order, but this is not always the case.

It is probably fair to say that things rarely go according to plan, and this process is something adopters describe as ranging from stressful to extremely distressing for both them and their adopted children. One parent described the assessment, preparation, and placement experience as "toxic". The parent also felt that foster carers had not appropriately managed their own sense of loss around letting the children go to their adoptive family. Other parents I spoke to felt that the overall adoption process was positive and supportive, and they were full of praise for those who recruited and supported them through to adoption. But even when the process has been positive, the beginning of the adoption journey can be fraught with worries and complexities for both the child and the parent(s), eclipsing the joy at becoming the longed-for "happy family".

Before working in the area of adoption, I worked for a perinatal service, and I encountered similar shocks and disappointments relating to the arrival of a child and things not going according to plan. A birth plan, like an adoption plan, is useful in that it enables the parents to focus on their ideals and takes into account their feelings, preferences, and fears and what resources and support the parents and baby will need. Unfortunately, many birth plans also get shelved during the fraught and risky process of bringing a child into the world. One mother told me about her disappointment and shock when she realized that the birth of her first baby was not going at all the way she had planned it.

She had intended to have a natural birth in a birthing pool, accompanied by her partner. However, after a very long labour, the baby became distressed in the womb and it became clear that urgent medical intervention was needed. The wished-for natural birth was no longer possible, and her partner was ushered away, as an emergency caesarean section had to be performed. What followed was a blood transfusion and a number of other intrusive medical procedures, meaning that she was separated from her baby for a number of hours after her birth. Even though her daughter had been born healthy, both mother and baby were reeling from the shock of this experience long after they returned home from hospital.

I have learned a great deal about how these difficult and traumatic starts for parents and children can stir up powerful feelings relating to loss, disappointment, and underlying fears of catastrophe. Group work is a sure way of putting you in touch with these key themes, especially a group that is full of troubled adolescents.

I would like to share my reflections from the beginning of a group session, which I have anonymized so that no young person can be identified. I have also included specific details about the importance of the journey before the start of the group.

Journey to a first group session

As I'm driving to the group from my clinic base I feel reasonably confident. The plan is beside me, and I have plenty time to negotiate the four-mile drive to the community venue where the group will be held. However, after about half a mile, I encounter a hold-up due to road-works. I turn round, but no matter how hard I try, every route seems blocked and inaccessible to me. I start to feel anxious and am concerned about being late, but I also begin to question my role in the group and the demands made on me in the running of these groups. I am feeling under pressure to provide a constant and containing presence for the group.

I take another detour, and this time I manage to get through, although I start to worry again, this time about parking and whether the parking machine will be working. I reflect on how exasperated I feel about there not being a suitable group room in the building where I work and the amount of travelling I have to do between work bases. I also find myself thinking about the lack of a secure base in my work setting. As I pull into a parking space fairly close to the group venue, I forget to be pleased that I am on time, that I have somewhere to park, and that my colleagues are joining me. Instead, I feel resentful and stressed and somewhat deprived. I am clearly "rattled", struggling to think about the task in hand.

Luckily my co-worker has the refreshments already laid out, and we assemble a circle of chairs and arrange the creative materials on the tables. I reflect briefly with my colleagues on my less-than creative state of mind, but together we are able to think about the experience of not feeling held during the transition from office to the group venue, the various demands on our time, and the drain on our internal resources. We manage to hear and contain each other's feelings with some humour, but also authentic concern, all before the young people arrive.

When the group members start to trickle in, we attempt to settle them into a rough circle with their chosen drinks and snacks. We talk about the need to create an environment where each person can be heard and will be permitted to think. But now that everyone has arrived, they are making a lot of noise, and there is a great deal of nervous laughter. We, the adults, think out loud about the need to listen to each other, and the word "respect" is talked about. It holds meaning for the group, but they argue about this while obsessively checking their mobile phones. There is then a jostling for position, and decisions are made about who should set the rules. There is a sense that those who have not found their voices are already starting to feel "left out".

There is a yellow foam ball on the floor. It has been a helpful prop in previous groups—it is soft enough not hurt or cause damage but can be bounced around to free up conversation and deflect some of the anxiety. My colleague speaks about the ground rules we have established and the fact that no one has mentioned confidentiality. She asks everyone what they think is ok or "safe" to share. "We're all adopted anyway", says one young person. "We all understand what that feels like."

Suddenly the yellow ball flies across the room, sending a drink flying. There is manic activity and hilarity. No one can find a cloth big enough for the spillage, "Isn't there a mop?" asks someone. I have a sense of chaos descending on the group, but eventually we establish who will clear up the drink and that everyone else will remain seated. I question how will we manage these kinds of difficulties and hear ourselves over the constant noise and threat of feelings spilling over. I also wonder to myself if our resources will be sufficient to hold the group. I say that it is so difficult to think, and how the mere mention of adoption, which is a common or shared experience for members of the group, has evoked a sense of anxiety, even panic. I also reflect on how everyone seems to want to avoid thinking, and that it is hard to remember why we are here.

My awareness that touching on adoption may have been "too much too soon" for the group allows others to speak about the noise and how they want to be able to hear each other. I emphasize the practical and solid reality of us all being here and the need to make space for each other. I also remind everyone of the dates and times of our meetings and when parents will be join us again. The group is quiet for a moment, and I wonder how it feels for the group being separate from their parents. My colleague and I give brief explanations about the need for belonging and acceptance, and then we return to how being adopted is a shared experience for everyone, but not something everyone is ready to think about. We acknowledge, too, that some group members are understandably communicating that they are not yet ready to reveal much of themselves yet.

"Miss" says one of the young women. "Is your hair for real?" This causes the others to laugh. "What is real?" I ask, reflecting on how this is a very important question for each of them in their pursuit to work out who they are. "Miss" says the same young woman, "just answer the question!"

Facilitating the group often feels like being responsible for numerous hungry and very noisy infants within adolescent bodies. They are all trying to find their voice and be heard. One of the facilitators shared with me after this session, that she had felt her jaw "aching with tension".

Despite the challenges, we as facilitators do "enjoy" observing the emerging individuality of each of the young persons in the group. When there can be an appreciation of lively encounters with young people within a group, it becomes possible for the individual to flourish. We also notice that, over the course of the group, the vocabulary of each attendee expands, along with increased confidence to speak about his or her experiences. It is as if the restrictions on the emotional vocabulary are gradually being lifted. These restrictions or censures are usually self-imposed, but, as they recede, other more powerful feelings can emerge.

Those of us who facilitate the group have witnessed how lively and challenging interactions are tolerated to allow space for bolder feelings of hatred and aggression. Initially these are feared, but they must be safely aired in order that they can be thought about and then contained. This environment is vitally important for these young people, but it can feel threatening to others, like parents, who are outside the group, in that it is markedly different from the more disciplined and restrictive environment of school or college.

Guarding against restricting the voices of young people who need to express their pain and to share their experiences, while also containing their desire to "know everything there is to know" about their birth history, is a huge challenge for parents. This is why gathering a supportive team around young people is so important. Equally important is the creation of spaces in the community where they can interact with each other safely while negotiating the process of individuation and managing a degree of separation from parents.

So Lyra and her daemon turned away from the world they were born in, and looked toward the sun, and walked into the sky. [Pullman, 1995, p. 399]

Adopted young people I have spoken to over the course of seven years of running groups say they need more safe places to express themselves without feeling judged or criticized. I am aware that there used to be more of these kinds of pro-social settings within the local community, such as youth centres and clubs. These are now a rarity, and the main social platforms used by young people are online.

In addition to changes in society around the way young people meet or communicate with each other is the pressure to look and be "the best" on these new forums—an added pressure to which this younger generation has had to adapt.

The generation born in 1995 or later, known as Generation Z, have grown accustomed to a world that is continuously changing and updating, which means that they have had to process information very quickly. According to Nosheen Iqbal (2018), who wrote about "Gen Z" in the *Guardian*, their attention span is significantly lower than that of Millennials (the previous generation), and they find it harder to focus. Anyone with a child of this generation can hardly fail to notice how many screens and lines of communication they can have "open" at any one time. They tend to use large group "feeds" or chats, and they stay in rather than going out to socialize. Many also prioritize their virtual identity over their "real" identity and will regularly document their lives with images and statements. Iqbal links some of the changes to advances in technology, but she also thinks they are responding to fears about their future and a lack of stability.

For adopted young people in today's society, the challenge is even greater. Those who feel that they exist "outside" the norm are at risk of exposing too much of themselves online. This can potentially lead to further humiliation and exploitation, rather than learning how to connect with others safely.

For this chapter, I have attempted to bring adopted young people's voices together to raise the most prevalent and preoccupying issues for them. What comes across very clearly is that they need much more help in understanding their histories and the confusing aspects of their lives in the here and now, but they are under such pressure to conform that it is hard for them to be authentic. They dare not risk showing their confusion and vulnerability within a society that has become easily distractible and preoccupied by what constitutes "success" or "failure".

"I wish that more adults would realize that even though we are young, we have had to grow up quickly. We don't have much of a chance to think about who we want to be any more—we have to spend our time trying to find ways to fit in . . . it's like we are always being watched and judged."

(YP, age 19 years)

CHAPTER SIX

The professional couple, the consultant, and the outside world

Robin Solomon

I am both delighted and grateful that Robin Solomon, an independent consultant and senior fellow of the Higher Education Academy, has kindly agreed to write this chapter. As someone I encountered while undertaking my child psychotherapy training at the Tavistock Clinic back in 2002, she inspired me to reflect on the dynamics within professional networks in a bolder way.

As a trainee with a caseload of mostly looked-after and adopted children in the service where I was based, and having no other psychotherapists to work with at the time, I knew that I needed to work out how to adapt in multi-agency networks while keeping a psychoanalytic focus for my work. There was also a fair amount of contempt for psychoanalysis in my clinic, and I found that I was constantly having to explain complex processes and ideas to stressed and anxious networks, who had little time for Freud or Klein or psychoanalytic terminology. To come across a social worker and teacher at this point in my training who could make psychoanalytic theory sound and feel relevant for my social work colleagues was a great relief and has helped me since to hone my practice, embracing a "down-to-earth" approach that is accessible to families and non-clinical professionals but without losing the framework and foundations of psychoanalytic practice. This is an approach that has been greatly appreciated by (most) professionals working with me, but also by the families themselves, with some of the most deprived and distressed children and young people.

Years later, I met Solomon again at a round-table event at Westminster, where adoption support was being discussed with reference to the rolling out of the Adoption Support Fund. A few service models were chosen to present their approaches, and AdCAMHS was one of these, although we were not being funded through the ASF. We described AdCAMHS as "a small service meeting a big need", but even back then there were other more glossy and "marketable" approaches being brought to the table.

I have continued to reflect with Solomon on the need for more consultation-based approaches involving social workers and families right at the start of an intervention, and how important it is to support partnership—an integrated approach to working with adoptive families. There is a real need to model healthy working relationships in the face of potential differences of opinion over treatment and support options, an approach that has been central to growing a successful adoption service model. Solomon understood the challenges immediately and was intrigued by our model, which aimed to deliver a combined approach to post-adoption support rather than one service commissioning the other to be the provider. This is something that managers and commissioners still continue to find confusing.

Solomon has since provided training for post-adoption–support social workers in Sussex and has consulted to us as service practitioner leads, funded through social care.

Most children adopted from state care have experienced breakdowns in primary relationships. This is not just the more recognized breakdown of the relationship between the infant and the mother, or primary carer, but also, fundamentally, the breakdown of the couple relationship that produced it.

R. D. Hinshelwood (2016) writes:

> "failed containing" may and frequently does occur, and then there is a sense of being uncontained—that is, at a mental level, an unconceptualized experience. . . . Failure is experienced as neither a space in one's own mind nor the possibility of space in another's mind, for something not yet understood or meaningful. Such a state is a kind of mismatch between the containing space and the thing to be contained. . . . These states occur in society (Bion, 1970) and in therapeutic groups (Hinshelwood, 1994) and probably also in couples. [p. 55]

Just as every child has two biological parents, so every adoption has required the input of more than one agency; but children's case files tend to focus on one parent at a time, often diminishing or excluding the other and rarely including a discussion about the couple which is more nuanced than "domestic violence". This is also the case for the legal, political, and organizational contexts, which replicate this single-lens focus through a process of task compartmentalization. We can think about this as an organizational "defence" mechanism, which in individuals is used to avoid the mental discomfort and anxiety aroused by having conflict within oneself and allows these conflicting ideas to coexist by avoiding or inhibiting awareness of them coming together. It might be helpful to think about this as an unconscious attempt to keep oppositional ideas in separate "mental rooms".

It is therefore not surprising that despite words and policies mandating that agencies and professionals "work together", under stressful conditions the result is often an aroused inter-agency anxiety, resulting in compartmentalized, disparate, and disconnected organizations and/ or inter-professional conflict.

Agencies and networks: professional homes

Authors such as Bion (1959, 1961), Jaques (1955), and Menzies (1960) discussed ideas about how groups may collectively share the experience of receiving unconscious projections. Ronald Britton (1981) introduced the idea of re-enactments when

> contact with some families may result in professional workers or their institutions becoming involved unknowingly in a drama which reflects a situation in the relationships of the family or within the minds of individual family members, and that this is not recognized but expressed in action. [p. 48]

Because all the workers are carrying out their tasks, it is at first quite difficult to see that these roles are being influenced by something quite powerful below the surface. However, Britton (1981) continues that this may

> eventually draw attention to itself by its repetitious nature or by the impasse which seems to follow a variety of initiatives. Indication of the presence of a prevailing unconscious process influencing profes-sional responses may be the intensity of feeling aroused by the case; the degree of dogmatism evoked or the pressure to take drastic or urgent measures. In contrast to this, the professional "symptoms" are inappropriate unconcern, surprising ignorance; undue complacency; uncharacteristic insensitivity or professional inertia. [p. 48]

Since Britton initially observed this, it has become more apparent how professional networks working with looked-after children and adopted children, removed and possibly re-moved because of family breakdown, get mirrored in the breakdown of the professional networks who should be supporting the child in new families.

Gianna Henry (1974) describes the child's first deprivation as abuse or neglect inflicted by external circumstances, which were out of the child's control. This produces a ripple of further deprivation as the child develops "crippling defences" in his internal world preventing him from making use of subsequent offers of support since he has come to experience others as potentially dangerous, neglectful, or unpredictable. As this is an unconscious process, the reality of the kindness or availability of others is not the issue; instead, the shadow of the previous relationships distorts how the child or young person experiences new ones.

These ripples extend further (Britton, 1981; Conway, 2009; Emanuel, 2002) to the ways in which the profoundly disturbing primitive mechanisms and defences against anxiety used by children and families get "re-enacted in the system by care professionals, who are recipients of powerful projections" (Emanuel, 2002, p. 163). An enactment is the doing of something in a concrete way that has not been able to be contained or metabolized through thought or sensitive attunement.

As in the early developmental process of the baby, a professional network wants to feel, be, or do good and rid itself of all that is "bad" (actions, feelings, etc.). Melanie Klein (1959) found that from the beginning of life a baby seeks contact with his mother/parent but wants only to take in good things, getting rid of bad things through the mechanisms of introjection and projection. This means that initially the mother is felt to be either very good or very bad. Some of the mother's "badness" becomes amplified if the baby projects his own aggression into the mother.

Klein called this stage of development the paranoid-schizoid position. The process of managing this complex emotional state has become known as "splitting" (1932)—the tendency to view events or people as either all bad or all good. These ideas about splitting and projecting, covered earlier in the book, have helped us understand the ordinary development of the infant and the infant–carer dyad. Klein developed these ideas further by referring to these early stages of development as "positions", which were relevant when working with adults in that she thought that adults oscillated between these infantile positions throughout their adult lives (Klein, 1932).

When we apply these ideas to networks, it can help us to understand why we have "anxious networks", where anxiety is introjected both from the organizational/policy/political experiences from above, and from emotional states re-enacted, as described by Britton earlier, from below. The network members are worried about blame, outcomes, or risk and therefore defend against these anxieties by splitting—viewing professionals as either "good" or "bad". For example, "good" professionals can be those who agree with the wider network or a particular perspective, and anyone who disagrees or who challenges the collusion can be seen as difficult, denying, or "bad".

If the anxieties of risk, blame, audit, competence, and so forth are unbearable (which in the current political and social climate we know they can be), the network displays defences similar to those used by the individual. In the face of extreme anxiety (such as being brought in to "fix" a potential adoption breakdown), professionals can fall back on the same type of manic defences as the baby, locating all of the good interventions, competency, and service resource in one agency or profession, while projecting all the bad into another. In this way, descriptions like "inept" or "unavailable" can also get attached to a professional or, more stereotypically, to a whole profession—such as social work.

Like splitting, denial is another primitive defence mechanism, which denotes a mental act where the reality of something we "know" is rejected because it faces us with potentially traumatic associations. "Disavowal", on the other hand, first described by Freud (1924e), is when the reality of the experience is accepted but the significance of that experience is minimized. For example, denial is when adults looking back on being beaten as a child deny or "forget" that it happened; disavowal, however, means acknowledging that it happened but arguing that it was somehow ok—and then going on to beat their own child because in their perception "it hadn't done them any harm".

This kind of remembering minimizes the pain, hurt, and damage and all the important feelings evoked at the time. In the same way, organizations faced with the push to minimize the effect of policy implementation that contradicts their historical values find themselves colluding with the disavowal. One example of this is when practitioners or their managers do not or cannot acknowledge how depleted and potentially "unsafe" their service has become, due to lack of resources being commissioned or to understaffing. This is because they know they need to accept the status quo and make the most of the little they have, rather than risk losing it all. This can be experienced below the surface as deprivation but can be very difficult to challenge in a culture where the majority seem to be accepting the deprivation and offering little resistance. When there is denial or disavowal, experiences can get re-enacted rather than understood and responded to appropriately.

In my own practice, I recall arriving at a network meeting where the professionals were due to be discussing a neglected child who had been received into care following her being locked out of her home and banging frantically on the door for hours to be let in, without knowing that her mother had abandoned her and their flat and had followed her new partner to another city, leaving no provision for her daughter. The current situation, when the now older child had not been given the key to her adoptive family home due to her irresponsible and risky behaviour, had evoked some of these painful memories, and on one occasion she had smashed all the windows, let herself in, damaged and stole property, and then later threatened her adoptive mother with a pair of scissors.

I had been invited to attend the professionals' "breakdown meeting", which I had had to squeeze into my diary. However, when I arrived at the venue late because of this, I found that there was no visitors' entrance, as it was a council office building that was not open to the public. Despite banging frantically on the door to attract someone's attention, I was not heard, and phone calls went to voicemail. Later, after not actually managing to get in and therefore attend the meeting, I was "denigrated" in the minutes, and the decision was taken in my absence to stop therapy, since this girl was going to be moved temporarily to a foster home. I was left feeling frustrated and furious, and the social worker who had organized the meeting struggled to mask her annoyance when we finally made contact. It was only through a later external consultation that the other social worker and I were able to appreciate that we and our agencies had, as Britton described, "enacted unknowingly a drama reflecting a situation in the minds of the child and family" (Britton, 1981, p. 48).

The paralysis often attributed to "disorganized attachments" and understood as a response to early abuse and neglect can also be re-enacted in the professional network, whereby social workers, police, and health and education workers become unable to make decisions when faced with the scary face of conflicting practice demands (i.e., respect the wishes of a vulnerable young person versus restricting the person's liberty; or, responding to emotional immaturity versus respecting the requirements of the person's chronological age). In addition to these conflicts, there are those that come from their managers or commissioners within different parts of the network, as well as through differing professional diktat. Paralysis in the professional or within the professional network could also be understood as a countertransference experience—a powerful communication via a projective identification of the child's experience of collapse in the face of contradictory states (Emanuel, 2002).

Steiner (1993) described a characteristic of what he called the "borderline position", where the mind functions as a defence, not only against fragmentation and confusion of the paranoid-schizoid position, but also against the mental pain and anxiety of the depressive position. Therefore, this borderline position acts as a safer mental space between the other two positions, where the person believes he can retreat if either paranoid or depressive anxieties become unbearable.

Professionals, on the receiving end of some of the awful experiences or emotional states of the adopted child, can find it hard to tolerate the mental pain they encounter. This is exacerbated by the anxieties that the current blame culture elicits, meaning that there can almost be a collective retreat into a "psychotic professional state" when making contact with these emotional states of the families—leaving everyone feeling quite "mad" with all that is going on. This can go some way to explain the ongoing need for a containing and reflective space in order to make sense of all that is felt, projected, and communicated within the professional network.

So while it is positive that professional organizations and networks continue to exist and try to function in complex and sometimes austere and persecutory environments, their capacity for providing receptive or nurturing care is further compromised when the complex dynamics of a traumatized or abused child also get projected into the networks. These stresses and consequent defences can then get enacted between individual professionals, who are susceptible, due to their own valences, to projections.

Building a strong house

I'll huff and I'll puff and I'll blow your house down.
The Wolf: *Three Little Pigs*

An understanding of these complex dynamic processes leads me to reflect on how difficult it is to construct and maintain a strong "house"— a secure containing space for adoptive families or those professionals supporting them—and to "keep the wolf from the door", as the old saying goes. Unfortunately the political response to adoption and provision made for adoptive families and the services around them can feel woefully inadequate—more like a house made of "straw" or "sticks".

At the time of writing, there is some support available through the ASF, and the necessary therapeutic interventions can be provided this way. However, statutory funding for grassroots services, that have grown to know the families through their difficult journeys, is constantly under threat. The ASF, rather than being used to furnish services that provide consistent and continual support, is used instead to fund private or charitable providers to complete assessments and treatment, but not to support the family longer term or to manage the risk as already highlighted. The ASF, in its defence, emerged in the wake of the growing awareness of the difficulties many adopted families were having after the initial "settling-in" or transitional period.

However, the complexity of the difficulties for some adoptive families and the resulting need has meant that a fund in and of itself has proved to be problematic in some respects. The commissioned time-limited provisions came in some circumstances to replicate a split-off, idealized service rather than a containing network that could manage the extent and longevity of the problems.

Some of the families I have worked with over the years in my clinical post within a specialist CAMHS adoption service conveyed feelings that adoption rhetoric was misrepresented, and the families often complained that they had been lied to or misinformed. Most of those with persistent difficulties felt aggrieved that during the adoption process they were told that the children might have difficulties due to their early experiences, but that after a few years, and with "therapy" or specialist help for the child as well as training for themselves, these difficulties would be "resolved", and they would become a "normal family". Some of these families therefore brought feelings of disappointment and betrayal to their sessions with me—like those already referred to in previous chapters—whereas those who spoke most highly of their adoption support social workers were often ones where the assessing organization had ensured continuity of the relationship with the original professional involved and the ongoing opportunity to be connected to the agency that placed the child.

The most aggrieved parents had in common the severing of relationships and the frequent changing of the professionals who were meant to support them. By the time I met parents, I was one in a long line of social workers or therapists who had already tried to help, or "interfered", only to then leave. The dynamics in the transference as previously referred to was that I would be scrutinizing their ability to parent and be ready to make judgements based on that scrutiny. I was therefore being unconsciously invited or provoked into recreating a relationship where I would become a critical presence who could shame them, or be someone who was so "out of touch" that I could not possibly understand the hell in which they lived. They were, however, able to explain that what they really needed were people who understood the complexity of their situation and that a "cure" was a fantasy, a desire rather than an actuality. They wanted someone who would, as one parent told me, "help shield us from the storm of adoption and keep our home intact". Another adopter said they needed "someone who would help with the plastering—rather than just paper over the cracks!"

The research of Selwyn, Wijedasa, and Meakings (2014) finally "evidenced" the extent of the problem. Perhaps the ASF was devised as a response to this increasing awareness of the extent of the difficulties posed by many of the children adopted following early relational trauma, coinciding with the government's commitment to adoption. The ASF appears to have evolved as the logical extension of a governmental and neoliberal ideology of privatization and commissioning based on competition. While extending and ring-fencing a budget targeted at increasing adoption—a theoretically laudable ambition coterminus with the prevailing dogma of moving public-care responsibility to the domain of individual or family responsibility—it set up a distribution structure that compartmentalized support frameworks. In essence, adoption support social workers employed by local authorities would need to apply for money through this government fund, which would be managed through a private company to pay for services, which would potentially be provided by the independent, charitable, or private sector. It would be disingenuous to avoid noting that the survival of some of these agencies in the current financial climate has become increasingly dependent on funding streams such as the ASF. The problem with the ASF model was that too often it commissioned time-limited interventions: the wallpaper model, which played into the myth of a "cure" for the traumatized child and/or family, rather than offering an ongoing, containing professional companion on the journey.

The regulatory framework of accountability for individual private psychotherapists was established requiring private providers to be Ofsted approved, as was already the case for private and independent agencies. Alternatively, they had the possibility of being taken under the umbrella of the local authority, which would be seeking the funding. Publicly provided services such as CAMHS or specialist NHS CAMHS services, or local authority provision already overstretched under austerity measures, were at the outset not eligible for ASF funding, and later they were restricted in what they could use it for.

I would like to suggest that the ASF became a systemic and structural manifestation of *compartmentalization*, the organizational defence mechanism described earlier. This design encourages splitting, offering an externalized structure in which to locate good or bad feelings, where separated agencies act as compartments unable to address or resolve the underlying conflicts.

While not-for-profit or private agencies and practitioners who had historically been developing models of excellent practice were being brought to the fore with this funding model and were viewed, often with good clinical reason, as holding much of the expertise around adoption support, this model of compartmentalizing or splitting up of adoption support is sometimes to the detriment of the expertise available within statutory services. As previously mentioned, many families who have been through a challenging assessment process involving the local authority adoption social workers, or with residual feelings about social work involvement in the early life or pre-adoption and placement phases of their adopted child, may well transfer those feelings to subsequent adoption support teams. The experience of engaging with those social workers is often already fraught with an adversarial template, so while the aspiration had been about working together, an unintended consequence of the fund has been the competitiveness that has emerged between organizations as a result of these tendering and divided processes. These splits and rivalries (Klein, 1937), idealizations, and denigrations resonate with the infantile experiences of the adopted children themselves.

At the same time, adoptive parents, a vocal and well-informed population, are researching their preferred providers through the internet or among growing support networks. They often see NHS services as "second tier", and they see social services, already experienced as "assessors" in the initial adoption processes, as professionals potentially obstructing their wishes and treatment choices. This model therefore potentially resonates with the grievances some families already have with the whole adoption process and the social workers charged with facilitating it. There is also the added difficulty of there not being a governmentally imposed cap on therapists' charges per session, so that market forces are potentially inflating the cost of therapy, and parents may even equate value and efficacy with the financial cost of the therapy.

So, while shorter commissioned services might have been helpful, and for many families it was sufficient or all they wanted, the model did not provide for the extended therapeutic interventions that were often necessary. The ASF commissioning model was not designed to set up longer term models of ongoing therapeutic support. Those families with the need or desire for continuing help—often the families dealing with severe mental health difficulties, educational struggles, or violent or self-harming behaviours—were then, in the words of many of the families I encountered, "thrown back" to statutory providers.

As a response, some organizations have been creatively attempting to join resources and create a robust coupling, working together, where different but complementary tasks are shared and valued. This is something I refer to in the second section of the next chapter, when focusing on the work of AdCAMHS, a service I have had the pleasure of consulting to and where I have been privy to the struggles that such organizational coupling entails.

However, local authority social workers, unable to commission sufficient ongoing long-term therapeutic support through the ASF, find that they are experienced as withholding or inadequate, and potentially even cruel, if they do not go with the private practitioners whom families have found. The subsequent need to resort to NHS/CAMHS services carries residual disappointment and the experience of being in receipt of something "not as good as" or "not good enough" (mirroring the adoption process for the child who may have experienced the adoptive family as not as good a family as the one formed through biological means). Yet at the same time, in the face of austerity, CAMHS are picking up some of the most complex and difficult cases—high risk, acting out, child-on-parent violence—at the point of acute crisis.

A further dynamic often enacted between the different agencies is where local authority services are blamed for commissioning delays and for service limitations but are not always privy to the efficacy of the different providers. Some are pushed by desperate parents to apply for whatever is requested and subsequently lose confidence in their own assessment skills; independent/private services, who may have previously provided helpful interventions, are generally not keen to manage a greater level of risk; NHS providers on the front line feel "dumped" with the worst situations without resources and are only able to offer brief interventions with patients who are angry, reluctant, and fed up with engaging in new relationships. This, albeit unintentionally, sets up a dynamic of disavowal or replicative deprivation.

While rationally this was not the intent of the ASF, and it must be acknowledged that there were statistically significant successful interventions provided, this compartmentalized and competitive model codified a structure ripe for splitting and projections internal to the clients, but then mirrored between the organizations and professionals. The links between the dysfunctional internal templates of self and other as embattled or competitive, idealized or denigrated, abandoning or inadequate—and the structures of the external world in the guise of the ASF—meet at the boundaries of professional practice in adoption.

In the various versions of the *Three Little Pigs*, the only way for the pigs to protect their vulnerability and outwit the wolf is to have a well-constructed and secure base or house and a well-thought out strategy. The moral is clear: there are no quick fixes and no easy way to build a house that can sustain the level of attack it is likely to be exposed to.

Keeping the couple in mind

The burgeoning use of attachment theory offered the adoption world a language and set of concepts that could be used by social workers, adopters, and mental health professionals alike. It was reputed to be evidence-based, and it provided some tools, such as the Adult Attachment Interview (AAI; Fonagy, Steele, & Steele, 1991; Fonagy, Target, Steele, & Steele, 1998) and Narrative Story Stems (Hodges, Hillman, & Steele, 2007; Hodges, Steele, Hillman, Henderson, & Kaniuk, 2005; Steele, Hodges, Kaniuk, Hillman, & Henderson, 2003), first in the domain of the birth families and the children placed for adoption and, subsequently, in assessing potential adopters; it even provided ideas about matching. Attachment theory came to be codified into policy and practice, in time rigidifying ideas that adopters should have "secure attachment profiles" and that the children would change their attachment profiles, often from disorganized or avoidant to secure, through adoption with securely attached adults.

This idea of an attachment template of self and other permeated adoption protocol. In a helpful way, this provided a shared language and a belief in the value of understanding early developmental experience. However, this "internal working model" conflates internal world to self and other—one in relation to the other. While helpful, it limits the necessary nuance to really grapple with the internal model of the other as a "couple in mind". For this reason, the more nuanced language of psychoanalysis can help.

At the beginning, the infant seeks a relationship with the mother (or primary caretakers), but inevitably it meets—and must meet for healthy development—with some disappointment. For example, when the mother cannot be available at all times or exactly when desired, or when the infant's distress feels too great to be managed. According to Fairbairn's model of psychic structure (Scharff & Scharff, 2014), "The mother who is beckoning without being overly seductive, and who can set limits without being persecuting or overly rejecting infuses the infant's self with feelings of safety, plenty, love and satisfaction" (p. 5). When frustrating experiences occur, the authors go on to explain, the infant can take into its mind this image of the mother as a mildly unsatisfying internal object, whether of an exciting or rejecting sort, and develops a way to manage the resultant feelings. However, when this occurs to a significant degree, identifiable as neglectful or abusive parenting, the infant is overwhelmed by these feelings and develops more rigid and limited ways of defending against these feelings.

Babies develop through a stage of omnipotence where the object is under their control, through to an awareness of separateness from the object—I am me, and you are you. While this is a necessary and healthy developmental achievement, it also allows for the painful awareness that the object on whom the baby is totally dependent *is also relating to others*.

Freud (1905d) presented this as an oedipal configuration. Although his use of Greek myth (and subsequently gendered associations) has met with decades of criticism, nevertheless what he was describing was simply the feelings of exclusion or inclusion that threesomes generate and the jealousy, possessiveness, and competition that this awareness engenders. However, in this way the baby develops not only a binary template of self and other, but also an internal template of this triangular experience: a self and a couple in mind. In this way, the baby also establishes unconscious prototypes of how couples relate to each other.

Significantly, the same phenomenon that happens between infant and parent later happens between couples. Bion (1961) described a spontaneous emotional fit, or valency, between individuals, which is about the complementarity between their unconscious needs. According to Dicks (1967), marriage (by which I include cohabitation or adult intimate relationships) can be understood as a state of continuous mutual projective identification. Becoming a couple relates both to the conscious needs, tasks, and roles each fulfils in relation to the other, but also to the shared unconscious assumptions and emotional fit between them. While cultural elements are the most obvious determinants of marital choice—the sharing of backgrounds or values that are part of conscious mate selection—Dicks' research shows that the long-term quality of a marriage is primarily determined by an unconscious fit between the internal-object relations of each partner (Dicks, 1967, cited in Scharff & Scharff, 2014).

It is important to note that, for most couples, this unconscious communication process functions helpfully in support of the ego. There are some couples, however, where the mutual projective identifications connect people in dysfunctional or perverse relationships. These are often couples where domestic violence, either overtly or through mechanisms that are coming to be thought about as "coercive control", cement the partners together in dangerous repetition of unsatisfactory couples in each partner's mind. Following on, for many couples the coming together of two produces a third. This union, whether joined through love or through aggression, leaves a ghost, a template of the way couples relate, within the psyche of the third.

Many of the children ultimately placed for adoption have internalized a dysfunctional couple. Often the conflictual relationship that created them ends with a rending of the couple—a leaver and a left. One position has as its heart the experience of exclusion from the couple relationship, where there is no room for baby in the complex enmeshment of the parental couple. The alternative is the experience of inclusion in an aggressive, cruel, coercive, or perverse relationship of the parental couple. Either way, the baby has internalized a parental couple who cannot work together, but who attack, abandon, exclude, or split. There is seldom an internalized couple who resolve and works things through.

In the experience and thus in the psyche of the abused or neglected child removed from these birth families for adoption is potentially a dysfunctional couple—a couple preoccupied with each other to the exclusion of the needs of the baby; a couple locked dangerously at war; or a couple where one partner has either abandoned or excluded the other. No wonder that the children of these dysfunctional couples, the children freed for adoption, although freed from the lived experience, can often bring with them rigid and implacable internal couples that cannot work together helpfully in the best interest of the child. In the process of caring for and "taking in" a traumatized child, the adoptive parents and other couplings around the child may also begin to "take in" the child's internal version of the couple who cannot work together and get drawn into this dysfunctional terrain in their interactions with each other.

Offering an "arms-around" holding: the nature of containment and consultation

Schore (2001), in his neuroscience research, discovered that affective messages are communicated from the right frontal lobe of the brain of one person to the right brain of another, below the level of consciousness. This had been theorized on a century earlier in psychoanalytic theory as the process by which parts of oneself are transmitted to the interior of the other person, where they resonate with the recipient's unconscious organization in a process of projective identification, which might evoke identification with the qualities of the projector. In other words, the recipient of a projective identification takes in aspects of the other person through introjective identification (Schore, 2001, cited in Scharff & Scharff, 2014, p. 7).

If you have ever been alongside a distressed and screaming baby, you will know how its distressed, anxious, or frightened feelings affect you. Likewise, as a consultant working alongside some "distressed and screaming teams", their tempestuous arguments or deathly silences disturbed me, triggered headaches or feelings of exhaustion, and made it difficult to think about what to say or do.

In the same way as the process that allows a baby to communicate its feelings to a receptive carer before it has the capacity for words or even thoughts, a team of professionals can communicate to a consultant without explicit words. The carer—or the consultant—is then called upon to take in those strong and sometimes extreme feelings and to chew them over and literally digest them, calling upon his or her own emotional capacity to withstand and filter those feelings as well as his or her mental capacity to process and make sense of them before feeding them back in manageable-sized bites, through an affective state of mind and responsive action. In both scenarios—carer or consultant—there is the move towards development of a shared "language".

Bion (1967) called this infantile process "containment" and described a continuous cycle of projective and introjective identification in which the parents' mind receives the unstructured anxieties of the child, which unconsciously resonate with the parents' mental structure, and then feeds these back in a more structured, detoxified way. This helps to develop a mental structure in the infant's mind. Over time, the child's growing mind is a product of affective and cognitive interaction with the parents.

Winnicott (1960) theorized that there were three basic elements to the earliest infant–parent relationship: the environment-mother, the object-mother, and the psychosomatic partnership. The psychosomatic partnership between parent and infant begins in pregnancy as a primarily somatic connection, with minor psychological aspects based on the parents' fantasies of their unborn child and their imagined roles as parents. The environment-mother offers an "arms-around" holding within which she positions the baby, providing a context for safety, security, a sense of well-being, and growth. Within this "arms-around" envelope, the object-mother offers herself for direct use by the baby in a "focused" relationship in which each incorporates the other as an internal object. Between the two there is a transitional zone that is in contact with both contextual relating and focused relating, and it is the zone that blends the two. Transitional space is also the space between the inside and the outside world for the mother and for the infant, and the space of exchange between their individual inner worlds (Scharff & Scharff, 2014).

> The British analyst, Denis Carpy (1989), added a further dimension to Bion's ideas about containment. He suggested that the baby not only projects but simultaneously observes the mother as she works to endure and understand the communication. As well as being contained the baby also observes whether the mother is able to survive the intensity of the bad feelings and how she is affected by the projections. [Solomon, 2018, p. 154]

The importance of appreciating the parallels between these unconscious processes and professional consultation processes became apparent to me over the years I worked with various teams. One staff team I consulted to was working with complex looked-after children, and the team's level of expertise and experience was very diverse. The consultation was in the afternoon, and staff often brought lunch. Some would comment on my not sharing their food. On one occasion, I tried to take a small offering, but I found myself choking as I tried to both talk and swallow. They would often throw around terms such as "attachment" or "projection", but in a rather superficial way that never seemed to be quite accurate, and I felt like the words were being lobbed at me. It felt combative, a way of different members competing with each other or with me, having to know as much as I or to reduce my usefulness, as if they already knew themselves everything I could bring. It often felt as though these words were being used to mimic, and I felt no real connection between the meaning and the experience.

As a result, I found myself pulled into "teaching" the concepts—although this sometimes felt like I was shoving the ideas down their throats. The experience felt bulimic, like a greedy feed that was then thrown up, without any space or time for digestion. Yet I felt very warmly towards these overwhelmed workers and wanted to put my "arms around" them. With regularity and reliability over time, there was more capacity to hold their anxieties and to tentatively put them into words, growing a more genuine relationship to the ideas and to the work.

> Bion found that people who have been deprived of emotional containment as a child project with great intensity when the opportunity is offered. [Bower, 2005, p. 11]

In much the same way, teams deprived of a containing experience, or where reflective opportunities are denigrated, can often feel either deadened or explosive. I recall one social worker arranging an appointment for a risky young person on the edge of placement breakdown. When we met, she apologized that the client would not come but admitted that she was relieved about that, because it meant she could use that time herself. Her manager would not have let her attend, had the session not been for the young person. Mocking a manager's sneering voice, she said: "Why would you go there? All they ever do is think, think, think!" After that, she became quite tearful, telling me that she thought she might be fired because her paperwork was not up to date, and then she sat in silence for a long time, until I was able to articulate the value of a containing space.

Previously, I had worked for two years consulting to a team where it felt as though the mainstay activity was to moan about other professionals or other agencies and their foibles. A great deal of hostility was generated towards these others, and the team seemed at their most convivial and like-minded when opportunities to complain about this other agency arose—but they would turn on me when I tried to notice this. Betty Joseph (1982) describes the extent of the hostility and the perverse gratification derived from these "repetitive ruminations". In her view, stuck, aggrieved people are caught in an addictive yet gratifying internal dynamic of accusing and blaming in a way that represents a destructive attack on themselves or on attempts at help.

Peter Blos (1991) described how the aggrieved service user comes to view him/herself as a victim and acts as if the professional or therapist is the perpetrator, inflicting the pain through his or her interventions. In the same way, it started to feel as if my presence at the team meetings was cruel, and that if I cared about them, I would either join in with their way of thinking or stop coming, as I was not doing anything helpful.

In this way, we can begin to think about grievance—first in the child, then in the adoptive families, and, finally, in adoption professionals and networks—as a possible response to trauma, where the repetitive complaint offers some gratification in itself. Interventions that might help with grieving, part of the ordinary emotional work necessary to manage loss and trauma, are rejected so that the grievance can continue protecting against the feelings of pain. This conversion of hurt to anger might be more helpfully understood as an unconscious defensive strategy to avoid feelings of helplessness or powerlessness, while the repetitive quality traps the aggrieved person into not knowing about his or her own distress (Solomon, 2018, p. 158).

Klein (1975) introduced the idea of envy as "the angry feeling that another person possesses and enjoys something desirable—the envious impulse being to take it away or to spoil it" (p. 181). Looked-after and adopted children may have a deep reservoir of envy in their external as well as their internal world. Many came into care because they did not have full access to a mother—both as part of the neglect of the early years and as a result of being in care. Those unbearable experiences feel and *are* unjust and can get managed through controlling and omnipotent behaviour. Envy and omnipotence can, then, therefore, easily get generated between the professionals, perhaps particularly between those tasked with an internal or external world focus: a careful eye must be kept to notice these if they arise.

Although I reflect in more detail on my consultations with AdCAMHS in chapter 7, I do want to highlight here how, in consulting to a project where the centrality of the partnership and the professional "couple" is overtly stated, the pressures to push the two apart allowed them, conversely, to join together and support each other. This professional home did not mandate living in the same room but having sliding doors between, so that the size and use of the room could be more flexible.

Otto Kernberg (1975) used the term "bridging interventions" for the therapist's attempts to straddle and contain contradictory and compartmentalized components of the patient's mind. The problem with compartmentalization is that it locks doors, inviting intrusive or excluding states of mind. The "bridging" consultant tries to ensure that the sliding doors are well oiled. Therefore, a model of consulting to such a professional couple must take into account the potential "rust" or door-track blockages between disciplines; it must highlight difficulties between theoretical frameworks and practice models and note fault lines of history and professional cultures. Dysfunctional professional couples are often dysfunctional because there is no containing process that encompasses all of the levels of potential disturbance in their functioning. This goes some way to explaining the need for the containing or "environment-mother", particularly when stress from the clients or the organizational systems attacks the linking of the professional couple.

To conclude, then, I would advocate for closer attention to be given to this kind of AdCAMHS model of managing the ambivalence, where uncertainty and complexity can be thought about and where adoptive families can feel held and validated, despite their ambivalence. This is a state of mind that can be hard to name and own, and managing this successfully often requires the presence of a third—the consultant—one who can have an eye on the professional and organizational contexts, above the surface. The consultant sits slightly outside the organization and can view the world of adoption and the policies and structures that surround it, while simultaneously keeping the other eye on the re-enactments of dysfunctional couples projected from the children and families: in other words, one who can also observe what is going on "below the surface" and pay attention, where necessary, to the internal couple each person brings to this professional marriage.

CHAPTER SEVEN

Establishing a psychoanalytically informed adoption service: the AdCAMHS model

with Robin Solomon

When I started writing this chapter, I became aware of how much I have come to rely on the support of my good friends and colleagues in building a service and developing a model that has relationships at its core. It incorporates approaches that may not be easy to measure, but ones that create a longer term approach to complexity and therefore allow the space to think and time to share difficult experiences and attribute meaning to them. I have therefore asked Robin Solomon who wrote the previous chapter, to join me in writing this chapter.

Section I, which I wrote very much from my own perspective, draws from the learning acquired over the course of establishing a local, integrated service model for delivering therapeutic and social work interventions for adopted children, young people, and their families (AdCAMHS). It also focuses on survival and how it can be possible to recover from the falls and to "land on your feet" despite the lack of resources or gaps in provision and the huge pressures facing services in austere times, where working closely together goes some way to providing the much-needed containment for families in crisis and struggling professional networks.

Section II was written by Robin Solomon as an outside consultant but with inside knowledge about processes of organizations and the tension and opportunities of bringing two professional cultures together to create a sense of security or "home" for adoptive families who had previously not "fitted" the referral criteria or remit for statutory mental health services.

I.   Making space: the AdCAMHS model

A man-trained boy would have been badly bruised, for the
fall was a good fifteen feet, but Mowgli fell as Baloo had
taught him to fall, and landed on his feet.

Rudyard Kipling, *The Jungle Book* (1894)

This chapter draws from the learning acquired over the course
of establishing a local, integrated service model—AdCAMHS—
for delivering therapeutic and social work interventions for
adopted children, young people, and their families. It also focuses
on survival and how it can be possible to recover from the falls and
to "land on one's feet" despite the lack of resources or gaps in provision and the huge pressures facing services in austere times, where
working closely together goes some way to providing the much-
needed containment for families in crisis and struggling professional
networks.

This first section of the chapter takes its themes from a previous
briefing I put together with John Simmonds and Caroline Thomas from
the CoramBAAF Adoption & Fostering Academy (Roy, 2017). The focus
of the briefing was to highlight the importance of developing service
models that bring together professionals right at the start of any intervention and the need, in thinking about adoption support, for a model
that includes social workers, mental health practitioners, and managers.
The briefing was written with the intention of informing commissioners,
and all those who have a responsibility for the planning or reorganiza-
tion of adoption services, about good practice with adopted children,
young people, and their families.

Most public sector services, even if they still have a functioning
multidisciplinary team, often do not have all the resources required to
meet these challenges and the multiple and complex needs of adoptive
families. Such is the predicament faced by many adoptive parents, in
that their longed-for children and their dream of a fuller family life has
placed a huge *strain and drain* on their personal resources and their relationships. This has left them feeling depleted and empty. Then, to add
insult to injury, the services apparently "set up" to provide the specialist support they need often do not have adequate resources available,
and these services may react negatively to the additional pressure being
placed on them.

As a model, AdCAMHS has helped to facilitate a more integrated
or partnership approach to adoption. This also provides an enabling

environment to address the exhaustion or "blocked care" described by Dan Hughes (2011). This is not only experienced by adoptive parents but can also be a very real issue for the professionals who work with them.

An overview

The AdCAMHS service model was established in 2014 in East Sussex to address the gap in provision for adoptive families, but it also recognized the stress levels of staff and so-called burnout experienced by social workers on the front line of adoption support. Its statement of purpose is:

> To support the best possible relationships and attachments between adopted children, young people and their parents/families.

Most of the clinicians who work in AdCAMHS are employed by the local NHS foundation trust and are clinically governed by trust processes, whereas the social work practitioners who sit within the service are employed by the county council. The service is operationally managed within specialist CAMHS but is commissioned and delivered jointly between both health and social care. Its core public sector workforce consists of one clinical lead, who is a child and adolescent psychotherapist; one social-work lead, who is a senior social work practitioner; a psychologist; a social care manager; and a part-time administrator. In addition, both mental health and social care provide service management from their respective organizations. Community and private sector workers are also commissioned through the Adoption Support Fund but are supported from within AdCAMHS. On the face of it, the staffing of AdCAMHS is minimal and even potentially inadequate for dealing with the level of complexity the service holds, but "The whole is greater than the Sum of its Parts", as Aristotle said. However, those of us who have been involved with AdCAMHS since its inception are surprised that it has survived as long as it has. Through working collaboratively across organizations, adoptive families report that they are, in the main, very satisfied with the treatment and support package that they have received.

All referred cases approved by the post-adoption support team manager are given a professional consultation appointment. The consultations are weekly and will include a CAMHS clinician, the allocated adoption support social worker, a manager, and/or a senior practitioner. Adoption support social workers select cases for discussion and provide their own expertise and reflection alongside AdCAMHS clinicians, but a consultation can provide the support forum they need and can be an end in and of itself, or it can lead on to a treatment pathway being offered. The treatment pathways are:

» *Individual therapy for children and young people*: Brief assessments and interventions or longer term for complex cases such as those children with attachment difficulties and disorders.

» *Specialist assessments for children and young people with complex and enduring difficulties and disorders*: These may often relate to neurological difficulties and disorders such as those caused by exposure to harmful influences in the womb. Children and young people with these difficulties and disorders generate the most anxiety in professionals and require higher than usual levels of professional experience and competence to manage and understand their complex neurobiological and relational difficulties, as well as the nature and severity of the risks involved in their lives.

» *Parent work and consultations*: This work can include other family members and/or involve specialist couples work.

» *Family work*: This enables the family and the network to challenge maladaptive patterns and processes such as splitting. These patterns and processes can also be addressed through more specific dyadic work.

» *Therapeutic parenting group*: This is a group course that runs for twelve sessions each year for roughly ten adoptive families, taking up to twenty adoptive parents. The group uses a psychodynamic model for supporting and training adoptive parents and builds on dyadic and attachment-focused models of group work. The parents are usually in crisis and require support from professionals and benefit from learning from each other about understanding behaviour. The course covers the theory behind children's developing minds, early relationships, and disturbance, such as the impact of early neglect/trauma on attachments.

» *Adolescent group*: This was requested by adopted young people and is run in a local arts centre over twelve weeks. It includes role play and creative activities as well as, at the end of each group, a woodland camp or outdoor experience with therapists, social workers, and forest school professionals.

Another of the AdCAMHS aims is also relevant here: the intention "to provide clear and collaborative recommendations for therapeutic interventions and to enable discussions about potential Adoption Support Fund bids to take place, ensuring that they are informed by clinical formulations" (Roy, 2017).

As a model, AdCAMHS aims to promote better relationships within families but also between professionals and families, through bringing together mental health and social care organizations, as well as preferred private providers, to work under one metaphorical roof, offering bespoke packages of therapeutic support and interventions for adoptive families.

However, as with most relationships, when it comes to finance and questions about who funds what and why, there are all kinds of potential tensions and disagreements to be managed before any collective agreement can be secured. There may also be differences of opinion over what constitutes a positive outcome for the family. In order to highlight the challenges of two organizations coming together to provide resources for the family, I shall reflect on the dated (and probably oversimplified) stereotypical and predominantly Western model of the parental couple. With this model, there would normally have been a "provider"—usually the father, who earned the wages and therefore brought in funds to meet the core needs of the family, such as food on the table, a home to live in, clothes to wear, and so forth. These wages were also important in other ways, such as for helping to create a sense of security and therefore maintaining a positive state of mind. In addition to these core functions of the family, the father's income would be used for the acquisition and therefore ownership of collateral and materialistic possessions, or symbols of success, which represented social standing and status in the community.

My understanding of this more traditional version of the couple is that there would have been different perspectives or definitions of what constituted core "needs" as opposed to being "beneficial" for the family—in other words, the non-essentials. In traditional families the father would hold the monetary power and would potentially be the one to make the big decisions about priorities for the family in terms of managing the resources. However, the mother, who was also a provider (but with less power in monetary terms), may well have had her own views about what constituted a need and would also be on the receiving end of additional pressures coming from the children. She would usually have been in a better position to understand these pressures and would in turn, have put pressure on her husband, interceding on her children's behalf.

She, too, would have to manage competing demands on her resources, while endeavouring to keep the emotional and physical temperature of the family home "just right" (like Goldilocks in the home of the three bears). She, the mother, would therefore usually have had the unenviable task of "keeping everyone happy". She may have wielded other powers, of course, but these were often focused on making sure she knew where the resources were coming from and how to gain access to them if she needed them.

It isn't any wonder that women who were trying to manage all these competing agendas and the pressure to hold everyone in mind (with few independent resources of their own) lost sight of their own needs and either became depressed and overwhelmed, or entered into conflict with their husbands. In some cases they left the family home altogether, as described by Elaine Tyler May in *Homeward Bound: American Families in the Cold War Era* (1988).

Despite the fact that this is a dated model for understanding couples, there are some similarities when it comes to managing resources and pressures across two professions and services and thinking about models for partnership. Such models can feel similarly dated for those who are trying to work on the front line and make sense of the constraints and what can appear to be random decisions about where the funding goes. As soon as resources become scarce, the potential for conflict and desire to control the other increases and the "harmony" is disturbed or at least sorely challenged. There is then the strong possibility that the individual partners will retreat back to their own culture or tradition and reject the relationship that had previously been mutually beneficial.

Power, like resources, has to be competed for, because funds are rarely accessible to those without power even when they know what the priorities should be. The struggle for ownership, and the competition for scarce resources, can be played out on all kinds of levels, turning services and/or their commissioners against each other. Unfortunately, families and staff members do get caught up in the crossfire.

In a well-functioning parental partnership, neither member of the couple would hold or wield all the power, as there would be an acknowledgement of what each contains for the other and for the family as a whole. Resources can be pooled, with equal access to a joint bank account, and there is trust in the other to manage precious resources responsibly. When these resources are especially tight, there would be a meaningful conversation about how the couple would distribute or save them, and denial would not be an option. There may well be disagreements about priorities, but these would be addressed and compromises made in order to find a way through this difficult time.

Unfortunately, professional partnerships can be more like the former arrangement, not in terms of being gender-specific or holding stereotypical roles, but more in relation to who wields the power and, more importantly, who has direct access to funds and the limited resources.

The ASF is one of these resources, which has also added further complications to the power and partnership dynamic. The fund requires the family's adoption support social worker to submit a bid for the therapeutic needs of an adoptive family, but these workers are not encouraged to reflect on what aspect of the work they might be able to manage perfectly well themselves, or to explore potential therapeutic resources within their own team. As a result, many social workers report that they begin to feel deskilled and marginalized. They may also belong to a team already feeling stretched and stressed and one where posts are being cut or frozen or are no longer part of the main statutory local authority offer. Like the nursery rhyme about the old woman in the shoe, the same could be applied to the isolated social worker: "She had so many children, she didn't know what to do."

So social workers apply to the fund to pay for external providers to undertake assessments and therapeutic work, paid at a good hourly rate. In many cases, the social worker will still be expected to continue to hold the family, manage the risks, and, as one colleague put it, "keep everyone happy, even if we are not feeling very happy about things ourselves".

These social workers will need to keep an eye on where the resources are coming from and notice when they might be running out, and they also need to be aware of any changes to processes when accessing the fund. What is more, they are expected to do all of this while keeping in mind all the many families on their case load. Any request made to the fund will be in order to resource families (or private providers), but the fund will not offer anything to them or their beleaguered statutory-funded teams. This unfortunately sets up a difficult dynamic in that their own professional family remains undernourished and neglected and even, at times, denigrated, while the families they support are being offered costly resources. Also, despite being social care professionals, they are made aware that they do not hold the power to make the big decisions themselves: they are not trained to make clinical formulations about treatment options but are expected to "signpost" families to other providers, commissioning outside services to do the work that they might in the past have been supported to do themselves.

As a psychotherapist, I have come to understand this dynamic more clearly when attempting to undertake work with adoptive families together with my social care "partners". This investment in the professional partnership has meant grappling with these dichotomies and power struggles, acknowledging the tensions but also owning my own sense of powerlessness in the face of shrinking resources within public sector services.

AdCAMHS has therefore adapted to this economy by extending its integrated working model and treatment pathways to include private practitioners, with appropriate professional registration. They have been woven into the fabric of the service in order to promote safe clinical practice and strong partnerships between public sector organizations and commissioned "preferred" private providers. There is redressing of the balance through agreeing a modest fee, but the private provider is supported with training and a group supervision arrangement. It also helps the post-adoption support team provide checks and balances for the work of these practitioners commissioned on an independent basis, but with clear treatment plans. As a model, it also provides a boundary and some protection for families who may feel desperate and pressured into making their own diagnoses and formulations without access to informed clinical opinions. This situation is far from straightforward for social workers who face frustrated families who see others receiving a particular treatment to which they feel they should have access. This dynamic or pressure also then needs to be thought about and shouldered together.

One of the hardest lessons I have had to learn in helping to set up a therapeutic service for adoptive families, and in working closely with social care colleagues, is that thinking alone is not enough. Nor is rushing in with a quick fix or a "tool kit" of strategies, which may even exacerbate the problem. There are times when a psychotherapist needs to roll up her sleeves and join the social worker in helping the family address significant risks, challenge neglect or maltreatment, and work together for the longer term to fight for the safety of a child or young person.

Thinking and "acting" in tandem has been vital in terms of continuing a meaningful partnership with social care colleagues. This does not mean that therapists have become social workers or that social workers have become therapists. What it does mean, though, is that we are developing a shared understanding of the difficulties and areas where we can overlap and appreciate our similarities and shared goals, rather than dwelling on our differences.

AdCAMHS's joined-up model therefore encourages all professionals working with a family to think together and to agree a plan, which can then be discussed openly with parents. The bulk of responsibility for managing the risk sits within statutory services, but the emphasis on partnership can potentially encourage other services, such as emergency duty and crisis teams, to come together around a plan.

The resulting shared investment in the plan produced through partnership enhances its chances of success, even if there are frustrations or disagreements. Making sure that the family has a voice within these professional conversations is not the same as blindly agreeing with their conclusions and applying to the ASF for any intervention that parents might have requested. One simple way that this can be managed is through centralized information sharing re assessments, risks, and care plans and any relevant history or contextual information, which is all gathered together before the start of any therapy or treatment. Parents are also, therefore, encouraged to contribute their views and responses to these plans but are aware that decisions can be made between themselves and professionals with all the relevant information openly shared at the onset.

All the way through the work, then, both social worker and clinician have the opportunity to work as partners. When this can be achieved, there is likely to be a better outcome for the referred child and their family. The temptation to "pass on" or to "let go of" the most challenging or complex families is strong, so any professionals working with the family are encouraged to attend reflective discussions, where they can explore the obstacles to working with the family. These discussions go beyond the usual case planning and record keeping and offer professionals valuable insights for their future work with families.

Communication is key and supports good partnerships between professionals from different trainings who hold different perspectives and can contain some of the most complex and chronic difficulties for families and networks. Good communication also goes some way to addressing the power imbalance, setting up a "shared bank account" of skills, training, and reflective resources. Understanding even the most critical and "blaming" communications, and being able to reflect on these as part of the work, is probably one of the most significant aspects of AdCAMHS, validating what each profession brings to the partnership.

The feedback from families suggests that the AdCAMHS holistic model for therapeutic and social work support results in families feeling more held and able to trust professionals. It also helps to address two widespread and related complaints made by adoptive parents about adoption support services. First, that professionals involved with adoptive families do not communicate with each other; and, second, that assessments are duplicated without necessarily resulting in much-needed treatment.

As a small service "growing up" in a time of austerity in the public sector, there has also been a mirroring within AdCAMHS of people's wider socio-economic experiences of deprivation and a lack of support in that AdCAMHS clinicians, along with the post-adoption support social work practitioners, regularly feel that they are left trying to hold a very compromised and poorly baby on their own, with very little in the way of resources or additional support.

AdCAMHS may not continue far into the future, but as a model it has the potential to establish a well-managed partnership-focused service, maximizing a small amount of resources to meet what appears to be a big and ever-increasing need. It is not without its flaws, but it does recognize the need for public and community services to come together as early as is possible in the lives of adopted children who present with relational difficulties and disorders. This approach can also lead to a reduction in the proportion of families arriving at the front door in crisis. Such cases are often harder and more costly to treat than those that are picked up earlier; or, as one parent explained:

> "We wish this service had been available sooner, when we really needed it. If AdCAMHS had been around when A was 5 rather than 13, we wouldn't be where we are now."

II.   Sharing space: the AdCAMHS model

When I learned about an adoption support and therapeutic service model developed in East Sussex in 2014, I was interested in how, as a service, it had been constructed but also in how these environmental and psychological (internal and external) pressures that stress professional "fault lines" would or could be managed. Being asked to contribute to this book on adoption, I have come to think more broadly on how this position might offer some ideas about the role and function of consultation to a professional couple and what it can offer to understanding adoption support more generally.

Aleksandra Novakovic, in her book about couple dynamics (2016), refers to the work of psychoanalyst Ronald Britton (2003):

> [I]n analysis, as in marriage, people share psychic space . . . the difficulties of sharing mental space in two categories of narcissistic patients. The borderline syndrome, which Britton refers to as "adherent narcissistic disorder", is characterized by the patient's inability to separate. There are "two people with only one mind", and there is a need to possess and colonize the other. The schizoid personality, or the detached narcissistic disorder patient, treats the other as if he or she were of no importance and excludes the other from his or her internal world. [Novakovic, 2016, p. 4]

The AdCAMHS statement of purpose prioritizes "integrating social work and therapeutic services" (Roy, 2017), the sharing of "psychic" as well as a physical space. As a combined service, its intention was to work across disciplines, support partnerships, join agencies together to work collaboratively with adoptive families, and straddle public and private divides. It was commissioned across sectors not only in order to assess and signpost, but to work together to provide efficacious clinical interventions where social care colleagues were valued contributors to any agreed plan and treatment formulation. The service specification emphasized that the model supported mental health and social care organisations working and thinking together, to provide tailor-made packages of therapeutic support and interventions for adoptive families. [Roy, 2017]

I was also drawn to their overt commitment to a model that "enhances social work practice". Social workers have increasingly been deskilled, as work historically done by social workers has been reallocated to others. I was therefore also heartened to see that "Social work practitioners are fully integrated into the team providing therapeutic support" and that "Their role is not limited to signposting children and families to other services. The model produces a package of care for adopted children, young people and their families which focuses on relationships."

The structural description states that "clinicians in AdCAMHS are employed by [the named] NHS Foundation Trust and clinically governed by Trust processes, while the social work practitioners who sit within the service, are employed by the local authority". Thus "the service is operationally managed within CAMHS Specialist Services while it is commissioned and delivered jointly between both health and social care".

Service delivery and development held between the two services presented, to my mind, some tremendous challenges. As a consultant, I had worked with services where one agency was commissioned by another, or where two teams had allocated and differentiated tasks. However, AdCAMHS set out to be jointly funded and jointly managed and to operate as a co-run service. This seemed ambitious in the light of the difficulties described when working together, so how could these agencies "work and think together" when there were internal and external forces huffing and puffing to blow the house down, as described in chapter 6?

Shakespeare describes the potential difficulties of a "marriage" between two different households:

Two households, both alike in dignity,
In fair Verona, where we lay our scene,
From ancient grudge break to new mutiny,
Where civil blood makes civil hands unclean.
From forth the fatal loins of these two foes
A pair of star-cross'd lovers take their life;
Whose misadventur'd piteous overthrows
Doth with their death bury their parents' strife.

[*Romeo and Juliet*, Prologue, 1–8]

Would a marriage of two different professional cultures or two households lead to the destruction of one or both, or could it bury historical strife and create an effective model? Does the joining of difference, as when an adopted family embraces an adopted child, lead to creation or to annihilation? There is the potential for both, but this *harmony* could only be achieved by maintaining a meaningful partnership between two professions and services, and this in itself would require significant work, containment, and support. This is also true when thinking about relationships and the couple—more specifically, the parental couple within an adoptive family.

I was first approached to act as a consultant by the AdCAMHS leads because I was a social worker by discipline and identification, alongside my years of experience as a therapeutic clinician in a specialist Fostering, Adoption and Kinship Care Service. I also held teaching responsibilities in applied psychoanalytic theory in a (respected) NHS Trust with both clinical and training functions. I think what appealed about my credentials was my having a "foot in both camps" and an eye to both of their roles—the adoption context and the struggle between the domains of the internal and external world in the lives and worlds surrounding adopted children.

I, in turn, was interested in how two statutory services could grapple creatively with reduced resources in a fast-changing environment and manage the impact this had on providing adoption support while straddling two professional systems (the NHS and the local authority). While it was a marriage between two services, it was a "mixed marriage", where each partner brought different history and background, customs and culture, values and ethics, language and identities.

Profound differences can generate anxieties, and this mixed marriage worried about the dominance of one culture over another and whether both cultures could exist safely together. Would one have to die to allow the other to survive? And could this marriage creatively produce a "baby" or project enriched by both parents, or would it, as for many of the families joined by adoption, suffer a painful and difficult amalgamation and potentially end in breakdown?

My initial reflections were about how two agencies, each with a different ethos and differing tasks and auspices, would communicate. Notably, one of the main things the mission statement affirmed as an agreed framework was that the model would be psychoanalytically informed—not the mother tongue of social work for half a century and overtaken by other psychological "dialects" in contemporary CAMHS. I was therefore interested in how the choice of therapeutic language would work across these domains.

Furthermore, stressing that AdCAMHS's work was not limited to direct clinical treatment, the service embraced the idea that the site of intervention included families, networks, and other agencies. It also challenged the idea that psychoanalytic thinking was limited to individ-

ual therapy with the adopted child or family. It called upon professionals to be reflective and predicated itself upon an idea that unconscious
communications could get mirrored in the professionals and networks
and would enhance practice, if these could be understood.

Like an attuned mother and baby, where language emerges as a result
of a shared understanding, the need for a shared language between
professionals working together seemed fundamental to the process of
professional attunement. External consultation might then entail helping
to decode and re-code different professional languages.

Responding to the request to contribute some thoughts on my consultation and on AdCAMHS, I found myself mulling over ideas about
couples and triangles. On one level, I was interested in the coupling
of two agencies and of two lead professionals through AdCAMHS.
However, by joining the lead couple as an external consultant, I also
found myself curious about consulting to a pair, rather than consulting
to a team, group, or individual, as I had done in the past. I wondered
about the experience of grievance that might manifest between a
couple working together in dividing tasks, workloads, having access
to managers, and whether the binary division between victims and
perpetrators would get located between them. The mainstay function of consultation was going to be, in my mind, to offer a holding
or containing experience (Winnicott, 1963). I had already come to
appreciate that agencies working together on joint interventions can
struggle with the act of getting help in the form of consultation and
often, like the birth family couples, can see those that help as being
part of the problem.

The AdCAMHS model included the role of the external consultant
right at its outset, in that it set out to use a consultative and collaborative approach to adoption support. Committed to providing a containing
and holding experience for those involved in adoption, it also furnished
the professional couple with the same resources offered to the child, the
parental couple, the family, and the network.

A mother with her "arms around"

As I discussed in chapter 6, Winnicott (1960) theorized that there were
three aspects of the earliest infant–parent relationship; the environment-
mother, the object-mother, and the psychosomatic partnership.

This psychosomatic partnership begins in pregnancy as a primarily somatic connection with resonance from psychological aspects of
the parents' fantasies of their unborn child and their imagined roles
as parents. This process was echoed in the way that my early expectations and anticipations of AdCAMHS were what one might refer to as

"gut responses" of excitement, pride, trepidation, and the vacillation between feeling well qualified and feeling inadequate. I envisaged my function as the "environment-mother" (Winnicott, 1960) who offers an "arms-around" holding, providing a context for safety, security, a sense of well-being, and growth. Within this "arms-around" envelope, Winnicott postulated, the object-mother offers herself as a direct object for use by the baby in a "focused" relationship in which each incorporates the other as an internal object. Between the two, he suggested, there is a "transitional zone", which is in contact with both the contextual and the focused ways of relating.

In principle, the consultations might offer opportunities for that "transitional zone", which, in Winnicott's model, provided the space between the inside and outside world for the mother and for the infant, and the space of exchange between their individual inner worlds (Winnicott, 1960, cited in Scharff & Scharff, 2014).

Often discussions in adoption support work are about the boundaries of confidentiality—what is public and what is private? What can and do you share with other professionals, and how to encourage agreement and participation from the family? In addition to these dilemmas, there are the sometimes conflicting obligations of different disciplines and professions around reporting, recording, and sharing of information. In AdCAMHS, I encountered a service that had developed beyond the initial partnership model to include private (closed-door) professionals into a "sliding-door" consultation service. The locus of intervention, too, had broadened, not only between the individual and the network, but beyond the consulting rooms in setting and in mind.

In designing the service, the lead professionals were from two different disciplines; as either observer or participant, I had been privy in the past to the dynamics evoked between social workers and psychotherapists: the idealizations and denigrations, the projections and identifications, the inclusions and exclusions, the blame and the grievances generated by working together and often codified into stereotypes and collusions. Perhaps a hope was that having integrated both disciplines in my professional self, I might help to mediate between these purviews.

At its heart, in every couple relationship, is the question of survival. This is also true of the professional couple. Can each professional survive the attacks from patients/clients and other professionals? Can each discipline survive, or will it be swallowed up by embracing the language and tasks of the other? Will one service dominate the other, and if so, will that mean that the qualities specific to each discipline and service will be lost? Yet, without the skills and knowledge of the other discipline as well as the shared potential to manage attacks and the anxiety, the work could become impossible and unsuccessful. A successful service must therefore live with such ambivalence.

The dilemmas of being in a couple are explained very succinctly by Cleavely (1993):

> At the very core of every defensive system and of every emotional conflict lies the longing for a close intimate relationship with a significant other, and of being a self-sufficient "I"—independent, autonomous, certain of being able to survive alone. The longing, however, is associated with anxiety. For the longing for closeness arouses the fear of being "swallowed up", taken over, dominated by the other, leading to a loss of self. The longing for autonomy gives rise to fears of being abandoned or being destructive, of survival threatened, and of the loss of the other. In the face of such conflict, ambivalence is born, and ways have to be found of managing loving and hating the same person. [p. 59]

Although my two colleagues often arrived to the consultations exhausted, this professional partnership stayed alive. The appreciation of what the other partner brought, and keeping that known about and articulated in lively conversation, was at the heart of our consultations. Each practitioner also had her own supervision and connection with her own management and governance systems, but the need to discuss things as a professional couple became a key part of maintaining the healthy connection between all the different parts or "positions" held within both teams.

At the beginning, each partner seemed to need slightly different things. The psychotherapist needed me to appreciate and acknowledge "the force of the blow" she faced, not only through the projections from families and complex challenging and often risky young people, but also both conscious and unconscious attacks by other professionals, including managers and social workers, and she very much wanted to contain these rather than react. What was needed was for me to acknowledge the injustice of these behaviours directed at her, to offer some explanation, context, and history as to why certain professionals might behave in a certain way, and to support her to face these destructive forces through my knowledge of the terrain.

The social worker, on the other hand, seemed to need a social work ally who also valued psychoanalytic ideas. While the psychotherapist spoke confidently in the language of psychoanalysis, the social worker found the language helpful but was more reticent about her knowledge and shy about using it. The double bind I thought she found herself in was that the more she embraced those theories and that language, the more she became identified with the psychotherapist, and the more she, too, started to suffer similar attacks. She wanted me to offer some training to the rest of her team in those ideas, and, while the psychotherapist could do it, it was felt that they might find it less threatening if this came from an "outside" senior social worker.

As time progressed, the content of the consultancy meetings often included thinking about the absence of protection from external forces. There was appreciation for those who had fought their corner to establish AdCAMHS; yet there were also moments of feeling the need to parent themselves, as managers were forced to face increasing external threats and demands. This space provided opportunities for managing the attacks and reparation of relationships—in reflection rather than in actuality. Early on and continuing throughout, I felt that I was in the presence of a thinking couple, a couple that appeared to enjoy being together but who at the outset were telling me about attacks on their capacity for creativity, coming from above and from below.

In the face of this well-functioning couple, I initially felt I had nothing to offer, or that all I could add were platitudes or sometimes some fresh insight into the outside world. What could they get from me that they did not already have? In fact, it again seemed evidential that it is the guarantee of a planned and regular thinking space that remains valuable. This couple knew this; their model had it at its core. From it grows a creative coupling where differences can be valued and appreciated and not something to fear.

Language as a tool for meaning-making, as thought about in the task of containment, may be a good example. A thoughtful decision was made to adopt the language of psychoanalysis—not through bullying or coercion, but because both partners felt that having a shared language was fundamental and that this language was acceptable to both. Had one of the couple rejected outright the use of this language, insisting on the use of a different language, this might have been the locus of conflict. Other dialects were valued and welcomed, but there was an understanding that the named language would become the mother tongue.

Although I came to this particular task with consulting experience, it was not of consulting to a professional couple as such. The importance of this has only become more interesting on reflection. Aware of the primary enactments that come to be mirrored in professional relationships, I anticipated that my work would be about helping to manage conflict. In the psyche of the abused or neglected child removed for adoption is potentially a dysfunctional couple—a couple preoccupied with each other to the exclusion of the needs of the baby; a couple locked dangerously at war; or a couple where one partner has either abandoned or excluded the other. Children of these dysfunctional couples, the children freed for adoption, although freed from the lived experience, often bring with them rigid and implacable object relationships of couples that cannot work together helpfully in the best interest of the child. These rigid and implacable object relationships get brought into the couple relationships of adopted families, and I anticipated the potential for this dynamic to be at the heart of the professional couple who had invited me to join. Knowledge and appreciation of the power of these processes might, though, have been what encouraged the inclusion of external consultancy in their model—putting in place a prophylactic structure.

In a previous individual consultancy to a deputy team manager of a service providing day care to young children who had experienced early neglect and abuse, I had agreed to focus on how the children's trauma was being projected into the team and how the staff were being affected by this. Many times my discussions with the deputy team manager related to tensions between her and her unit manager. We reflected on the psychic (and sometimes physical) attacks from the children on her and her unit manager as a functioning couple, as was my brief, but I was gradually becoming aware of actual tensions described between the two, around task allocation, authority, and responsibility. Although there was a great deal of what I am sure was genuine respect and appreciation of the unit manager, I was increasingly left feeling as if I was witness to belittling or bullying. What sounded like unreasonable amounts of work were allocated, leaving the deputy manager unable to complete all her tasks. Yet she often described not feeling "good enough".

Although she had originally requested consultation because she understood its value, there was an organizational idea that she was the "weak" or inadequate one who needed help, while the unit manager was the one who could cope very well on her own. I kept suggesting that the two of them should seek joint consultation, because something was not functioning helpfully between them. However, it was not possible to bring the two together, and the consultations came more and more to feel stuck; I felt that I was being invited to witness an abusive dynamic.

While this was a re-enactment of the children's dramas, what also needed attending to was the couple and the complex dynamics that came from the organizational structure and the internal templates of couples that was making this working partnership dysfunctional. The AdCAMHS model, however, appreciated that both members of the professional couple had to be equally committed to the consultation process for it to be effective.

Arriving from different tasks or places at the end of a working day to the consultation venue, which itself was interesting—a quiet but public space where coffee and refreshments were available and became a regular feed—we were often first two, before three. In hindsight, it is interesting that if the other person was the social worker, almost from the outset it felt acceptable to spontaneously hug—as if the social work culture could accommodate the actual hug, knowing it embodied a genuine pleasure of meeting, while needing, of course, to be mindful of evaluating the appropriateness of physical touch. With the psychotherapist, on the other hand, at first I was more tentative—not because I felt less pleasure or less warmth towards her, but perhaps, less consciously, enacting one of the tensions between the two disciplines—acting meaning versus naming meaning: as if I ought, instead, to say how we both noticed the desire for a professional embrace.

Unpicking this, it was not the more commonly attributed difference between doing versus thinking, but, rather, the social work skill of demonstrating receipt of a communication through an action replay rather than through an interpretation. It was before the long summer break that she and I finally made a move towards each other to hug, laughing at the momentary awkwardness of a truly "arms-around" moment before it was achieved. I think we all enjoyed a moment of recognition of this new shared model being forged together.

When three people sit together, it is impossible for one to look directly at both of the others simultaneously, although both can look at the third. The direction of the gaze and the experience of being gazed upon can resonate with the templates of the couples we hold in our mind. At moments, the third can experience a feeling of exclusion; at other times, she or he may feel benignly looked upon by two. Later, this couple-in-mind may ensnare us to enact these positions.

As I came to understand this working-couple dynamic better, I became more conscious of the direction of my gaze and the need to keep both perspectives and professions or parent organizations in mind. I became self-conscious when the social worker in me joined the social work partner to look at the psychotherapist, and at other points how my clinical self partnered the psychotherapist to look at the social worker. At times, I became aware of identification, through envy, idealization, or shame, for example, but at others it was to lend support to one role or another when it felt under attack. Utilizing a more conscious awareness of this "third position"—which describes how initially the child develops a capacity to be a participant in a relationship, observed by a third *and* being an observer of a relationship between two people (Bion, 1962b; Britton, 1998; Steiner, 2011)—allows this to offer us clues to the relationship between the others.

Somewhat to my surprise, and pleasure, but perhaps because we were aware of how these common dynamics came to be enacted and also trusted a model that had anticipated them, I encountered a well-functioning and productive couple. Dysfunctional professional couples are often dysfunctional because there is no containing process that encompasses all the levels of potential disturbance to their functioning. There needs to be an eye to the professional and organization contexts, in this case the world of adoption and the policies and structures that surround it. There needs to be an eye to the re-enactments of dysfunctional couples in the child and families. And there needs to be some attention, where necessary, to the internal couples each person brings to the pair.

I hope, therefore, that my reflections on being a consultant to a professional couple at the heart of a service where pairing and partnerships are central might add to an understanding of how to support families with complex challenges, and that it may also help to strengthen those services that relate to them. I would even go so far as advocating for extending the AdCAMHS statement of purpose—"to support the best possible relationships and attachments between adopted children, young people and their parents/families" (Roy, 2017)—to include relationships with and between professionals.

CHAPTER EIGHT

Baby number 9: let's talk about the birth parents

I have an inward treasure born with me, which can keep me alive if all extraneous delights should be withheld, or offered only at a price I cannot afford to give.

Charlotte Brontë, *Jane Eyre* (1847)

Being adopted or removed from birth parents is unlikely to be the only traumatic event an adopted individual will experience, but such a primary loss is bound to have lasting significance well into adulthood. Over the course of writing this book, I have attempted to set out how our histories influence our choices, whether we are adopted or not, and how, in adulthood, we may well look back with surprise and notice how unseen "forces" or "inward treasures" have shaped us over the course of our lives. Because these "forces" are beyond our conscious awareness, however, we may struggle to understand them or connect them to who we are in the present.

Freud (1915e) and other pioneers in psychoanalysis were interested in these unseen or unconscious processes and how our childhood experiences and earliest relationships influence our behaviours and feelings well into adulthood, leading us down certain paths while drawing us away from other possible ones. More recently, others, like Allan Schore (1994, 2001, 2012) and Jonathan Shedler (2010), have come to understand more about where these experiences are stored or located in the brain. Schore explains that the brain is divided into two hemispheres, right and left. The right hemisphere is the domain of non-verbal emotion, imagery, and what Schore calls "implicit procedural memory" and intuitive knowledge. It is also the part of the brain where memories are laid down even before the development of language—in infancy—and therefore where the "unconscious" resides. Shedler argues that even the term "unconscious" is difficult for some to comprehend, but that memories and perceptual as well as affective processes are not consciously accessible to us.

Over the years of my training, working as a psychotherapist and having my own psychoanalysis and clinical supervision, I have become aware of how our histories and childhood experiences can also influence (consciously or unconsciously) our choice of profession. This is perhaps more noticeable for those working within the helping or "healing" professions, where there may be an underlying motivation to help or heal others, in order, perhaps, to help or heal ourselves. Some may also have been drawn to a career focused on caring for others or understanding their behaviour because, as children, they were required to take on a caring role within the family or had to learn how to be receptive to changes in their parents' state of mind.

For child psychotherapists, psychoanalysis is a core part of their training, as well as having regular face-to-face supervision. One of the positives of this provision, which happens alongside the training, is that it affords trainees the opportunity to understand or become more consciously aware of any difficulties or feelings they may have themselves, relating to their past experiences. It also means that trainees should be more able to differentiate between their own and their patients' difficulties.

I have come across a number of colleagues in adoption-related work who respect and admire this aspect of a psychoanalytic training and have recognized their own need for therapy, because of what their work stirs up within them. Some of these colleagues have themselves been adopted and have understandably been drawn into adoption-related work, but they are still surprised and even shocked by feelings and memories that can "surface" as a result of working with this client group.

In this chapter, I want to draw from the perspective of a colleague (B) who is also an adopted adult and whose professional role involves working closely with birth mothers who have had babies removed and taken into care or placed for adoption. B has generously agreed to share her reflections about her own history and how she came to realize that being relinquished by her own birth mother had significantly influenced her choice of career.

Many of the mothers B works with continue to get pregnant in the hope that they will keep one of their babies, but, instead, they end up experiencing the loss of more babies, as they are taken away or repeatedly removed. Being in contact with a highly distressed parent–infant couple who are likely to be separated is an area of work that could feel too hopeless or upsetting for many professionals, even for those who are used to working with families where there are safeguarding concerns. I was therefore curious about why B felt so drawn to this work.

"I started out as a clinical nurse specialist, but I always had an interest in mothers and babies. It is interesting how I have ended up developing a role within a project that works with birth parents—mostly mothers, who have had their babies or children forcibly removed. I know that relationship-based practice has always been important to me, but I feel especially invested in helping parents to build better relationships with their children. I do know that this is because I was adopted as a baby, as my birth mother decided to give me up—even before I was born. It's hard to know the real reason behind her doing this. I think I always wondered why—but I also wanted to understand, that's the main reason. My birth mother was in a relationship with someone at the time who actually wanted her to keep me, and I know that her family would also have supported her. She could have kept me, but she didn't, and I'll never really understand that. Maybe she just wasn't ready to build a relationship with me and therefore chose to let me go. I'm probably still trying to make sense of this."

Relinquishing a child was more common for past generations, where it was frowned upon to have a child "out of wedlock", meaning that there were more babies relinquished by their birth mothers and placed for adoption. Society has changed considerably since B was adopted, and, thankfully, babies are not removed from parents due to marital or financial status and are also less likely to be willingly given up by healthy young mothers for adoption. This change, however, does mean that many of the babies or children who are placed on the adoption register are the children of parents who have significant mental health difficulties, a history of domestic violence, experience of physical or sexual abuse or substance misuse, and may have been in the care system themselves. These babies have mostly been removed (rather than relinquished) because it would not have been safe for them to remain with their birth parents.

For adults who want to adopt a child, the process is also much more complicated than it was when B was adopted. Any adult who wants to adopt will first need to contact a regulated and approved adoption agency, which may be part of the local council or a voluntary agency. Once the agency gets an application, it will begin adoption preparation for prospective adopters, who will be invited to attend a number of "prep" classes. These are normally held locally and offer advice about what to expect from the process and what adopting a child could be like—as well as the potential challenges. After the preparation stage, a social worker will visit prospective adopters in their home and complete a detailed assessment. The assessment should include questions about adopters' childhood experiences and family histories, and there will usually be questions about key attachments and any issues affecting the parental couple relationship. Police checks and references will also be carried out, as well as full medical checks.

Once the assessment report is complete, it is sent to an independent adoption panel, which makes a recommendation to the adoption agency. This recommendation will be considered by the agency, and a final decision is made about whether would-be adopters are suitable to become adoptive parents. If approved, the process of finding a child (whose name is on the adoption register) will then begin in earnest.

Although adopters say that this process is rigorous and emotionally draining, there is usually emphasis placed on the importance of understanding the child's birth history and on educating adopters about how to think this through together so that they can talk about it with their adopted child or children at a later stage. This experience varies from one authority to another, and some adopters say they weren't prepared for what adoption stirred up for them as a family, or that they weren't made aware of how much the early history of the child would affect their later lives. Others felt that the preparation was helpful and realistic and that they were given an honest picture of how things could go and what might need to be shared with their child. However, most say that the information was focused more on the early stages of adoption.

A good number of adopters I have spoken to over the years of working with adoptive families say that they weren't given an indication that the difficulties could go on "forever" and that there wasn't enough emphasis on the future or where to get help if things go wrong.

B feels that, overall, the changes to the process that have been introduced since she was adopted are positive, and she wished her adoptive parents had been assessed the way parents would be today, especially the bit about being encouraged to talk with B about her birth history. Adoption assessments, she feels, are much more thorough now, helping prospective adopters to understand more about why they want to adopt and what it will involve, but also about how the baby or child is likely to be affected by the loss of the birth parents. She emphasized the importance of early intervention and additional services being available to support birth mothers—especially those who are struggling to keep hold of their babies.

> "In my work, I see a different picture to how things were for me. I support mothers who, despite their complex difficulties and painful histories, are desperate to keep their babies. They don't want them to be taken away—they want to hold on to them. I have worked with many mothers who have had repeat removals, but also some mothers who eventually, with a lot of help, get to keep their babies. I have been supporting one mother who is currently providing good care for her baby—she has managed to hold on to him for the longest time, and things are going well. This one is *Baby number 9!*"

Writing about this feels complicated on all kinds of levels, for I am only too aware how many adopters feel about neglectful birth parents, having found the process of trying to conceive a child themselves extremely problematic. After potentially undergoing numerous unsuccessful rounds of IVF, some adopters feel extremely fragile, but, in order to adopt, they have to undergo an intensely rigorous assessment. They understandably feel that this situation is unfair—especially when they know that there are birth parents who continue to have babies that they will neglect or hurt or, at the very least, fail to protect. And yet they receive support to potentially help them keep their babies. This feels provocative to adopters and can reignite their own smouldering feelings relating to loss and childlessness.

I talked to B about this and the potential ambivalence. I also wondered what the main focus for the work with mothers who have had repeat removals would be. Could anything be done to help them change the cycle of neglect, abuse, and rejection? B understood the desire to challenge the behaviour of a neglectful birth mother, but she emphasized that this isn't the best starting point for the work.

> "Although we focus on the reasons for repeat removals, we don't start by challenging the mother's behaviour, that comes later—we work first on building a secure-enough relationship with her. She has often experienced neglect or has been rejected herself as a child. We will also work with the baby's father, if he will engage with us."

She explained that she would address the problems from a number of angles, such as sexual health, to prevent further pregnancies (where possible, until the work is completed) and to build a stronger network of support around a mother who has been very alone but may have also chosen to isolate herself from others.

"We start by listening, and building a connection, but we also look at why certain behaviour patterns are being used. For example, many mothers who have 'lost' their babies will self-medicate. The loss of a baby or numerous losses is too much for them to bear, and they resort to drink and drugs to deaden the emotional pain. Or they try to deal with the loss by seeking to replace the lost baby with another."

With regard to Baby number 9, B explained that this mother had experienced long-term domestic abuse but had also continued to seek out relationships with men who controlled or dominated her. She did not seem to have the internal resources to be assertive—and therefore was not strong enough to protect herself or her babies. This only caused deeper feelings of low self-esteem, coupled with self-hatred, which perpetuated the cycle of neglect and rejection.

Every time another baby was removed, the mother would sink deeper into despair, where her infantile feelings of distress and unmet needs surfaced. However, after two years of work with B, beginning very gently at first and establishing a predictable pattern of one-to-one support (like that of a receptive mother with her new baby), B started to notice changes in the interactions between mother and baby. She also set up positive social opportunities for this mother to build new connections with others and encouraged her to experience her own and her baby's body in a new way, such as through attending mother-and-baby groups and yoga classes.

As I write this, I am also reminded of all the valuable early intervention work with the parents and their babies through parent–infant psychotherapy (Salomonsson, 2014) and how intercepting difficulties as early as possible can make a huge difference to the quality of the attachment between mother/parent and baby (Health and Social Care Committee, 2019).

The importance of how a parent communicates and relates to his or her infant can be observed in the "still-face" procedure or experiment (Tronick, Adamson, Als, & Brazelton, 1978; see also Adamson & Frick, 2003). It shows how a baby responds when her mother (who has been interacting normally) suddenly changes and holds a still or expressionless face. The baby picks up on the still face immediately and communicates that she knows that something is wrong. Confusion is quickly followed by distress and then a turning away from the still face—trying to switch off from the lack of responsiveness from her mother and pretending it isn't happening. The baby is also visibly relieved when the mother finally "returns" and reassures her.

This experiment can help us to understand the relationship between a professional and a vulnerable birth mother/parent in that, if the professional stops being lively and available and instead presents a "still face" through being unavailable, then the birth mother will respond in much the same way as the baby in the still-face experiment. She may start by showing her frustration or even rage at not being responded to, but then becomes confused and distressed, finally turning away herself or "closing down". I have heard a number of chronologies relating to an adoption where a vulnerable birth mother who is being supported within a mother-and-baby placement coincidently walks out, abandoning her baby, at the point when the carer "popped out" to the shops or became unavailable in some way.

The way that vulnerable (young) birth mothers behave towards carers or professionals, such as social workers, who, they feel, have turned away from them, is through initially being hostile or confrontational. This is usually followed by avoidance of meetings, not returning calls, and even failing to attend important appointments, either for them or for their baby. Rather than this being understood as a response to what feels like the professional's still face, they are, instead, viewed as placing themselves and their baby at greater risk.

On occasions when I have been asked to support an adopted young person who has had a baby, I have encountered the same pattern of turning away in response to what is felt to be unresponsiveness from the professional, who has not recognized the mother's desperation or fear or who has suddenly left or handed her over to another professional. Unfortunately there are too many young people who have had to endure numerous changes in social worker and/or foster placements at really difficult or crucial times in their lives, when what they really needed was someone who would be willing to provide some consistent care and who would remain interested in them and curious about the change in their behaviour.

The modelling of a lively and in-tune responsiveness, by staying present but putting clear boundaries and appropriate assertiveness in place, was vitally important for the mother of Baby number 9, and it facilitated her capacity to take in positive resources. For the first time, she started to feel that her distress was being noticed and attended to. Therefore, rather than closing down, which she had done on previous occasions, she managed to stay connected to B (and to her baby) and resisted the desire to switch off or escape.

Establishing a trusting relationship through the provision of regular therapy was a big part of this process and allowed the significant trauma and past abuse to become more known about (conscious) and therefore to be treated. Rather than being continually acted out through rejection, addiction, and denial of the infantile part of herself (which had previously resulted in losing her babies), this mother had become more attentive to the neglected child within herself.

B talked to me about how one of the biggest challenges for the mother of Baby number 9 had been her impaired capacity to mentalize. She could not put herself in the position of others and relate to their feelings—something that her baby would have needed from her in order to be and feel safe. A mother needs to be able to put her own preoccupations to one side in order to care for her infant and understand his or her pressing needs.

Mentalization is something most of us use in our everyday lives to a greater or lesser degree in order to relate to others. However, some people find it more difficult to do, especially in more intense or pressurized situations like intimate relationships, where feelings are powerful and can be extremely difficult to regulate or control. Treatments that aim to restore the capacity to mentalize through establishing a safe attachment relationship with the therapist have been developed, such as mentalization-based therapy for adults (MBT; Bateman & Fonagy, 2004), and mentalization-based therapy for children or young people (MBT-C; Midgely & Groove, 2012).

B advocates using these approaches with patients who struggle to mentalize or empathize, but she also reflects on the importance of a professional being able to mentalize themselves and use whatever resources are available to them to address their own areas of difficulty, especially around relating to others. Going over her own history had been hard, but it had been necessary in order to feel able to focus on the needs of these mothers and their babies. This reflective capacity and being able to understand their plight without being too caught up in their distress was only possible through having the opportunity to discuss her own history and feelings in a therapeutic space and through her having reflective, clinical supervision.

"I realized that I had questioned my identity and self-worth over the years, because I knew that I was relinquished—it felt hard for me to exist in my own right."

As an adult, B had learned to find the courage to do something about her curiosity relating to her past and had formally requested her adoption records. She was given or sent lots of information, but it did not arrive in an orderly fashion. Instead, everything—letters, court documents, photos, and so on—arrived in "bits and pieces". It was hard for B to make sense of them and to know how to bring these precious fragments of her life together. She described how she eventually "gathered it all up" and put it into a scrapbook, collating all the bits of information in her own way, a kind of re-working or re-telling of her story. However, she didn't really know what to do with it next. It had become a "patchwork quilt" of a story that she couldn't wrap around herself proudly but, instead, felt obliged to keep hidden, especially from her adoptive parents.

We talked about how B understood the need in others to keep aspects of themselves hidden and how she had not felt able to be truthful with her adoptive parents about finding out about her birth mother, or that she still had a secret yearning and a determination to find her.

> "There was something in the pile of stuff that I kept going back to—it was a letter from my birth mother, which she wrote for me just before I was adopted. She set out her reasons for giving me up—such as wanting me to have a better life and to be loved and happy. It's strange, though, how clear she was that I wouldn't get any of this from her, and that a 'better life' meant being without her. . . . How could she know? It was this letter that kept drawing me back to her—it was so neatly written and well put together, and seeing her handwriting, I could almost hear her voice and feel her speaking to me."

B also reflected on the "draw" from her birth mother and her desire to find out anything she could, but also how this felt confusing, and she feared that she may have betrayed her adoptive parents by even having these feelings in the first place. Her curiosity eventually led her to proactively seek out her birth mother—interestingly, after she had had her own children.

> "When my children were little, I decided I would find her, and so I did some digging. I managed to find the name and phone number for the place where she used to work, and I called up, saying that I was trying to trace someone (and gave her name). I also said that I wanted to let her know about a reunion. Someone there knew who she was, and gave me a number. When I called that number, my birth mother answered—it was that simple. When she heard my voice, she told me that she had been waiting for my call for 27 years!"

Of course, the process of finding her birth mother was not really that simple, and although B arranged a meeting, her birth mother was ambivalent about having continued contact and did not want her other children and family to know about B. Equally, B didn't want her siblings or her adoptive parents to find out.

"They couldn't know about it, they wouldn't have been happy. I think they would have rejected me."

This fear (sometimes irrational) of rejection is a common phenomenon for those who have been adopted, and it generates sadness and a deep sense of loneliness, something B could relate to. She spoke of times where she felt that she didn't really belong with either family—a predicament that other young people and adults who are adopted have described to me, in that whichever path they choose, they are aligning themselves with either their adoptive or their birth parents. Feeling caught between these two different worlds or paths can cause a paralysis for the adopted young person or adult and lead to feelings of despair and confusion about their identity. B realized that her adoptive mother didn't want people to know about the adoption, just as her biological mother hadn't wanted people to know about B's birth.

"My birth mother hadn't wanted to keep a baby out of wedlock, so she kept my existence hidden. I think she thought she could just carry on her life without me. She went on to have other children and didn't tell them about me. So I discovered that appearances were very important to my birth mother, but, looking back, I can see that they were also important to my adoptive mother, too."

I asked B about the proliferation of secrets within both her families and how this can happen in families, but especially in adoptive families. She agreed and talked about how her birth-history "scrapbook" represented something to her about the need for her real-life experiences and history to be known about but, at the same time, the desire for it to be hidden away and kept safe. She thought that this was why she had put it in the boot of her husband's car for years, out of a fear that her adoptive parents might feel betrayed if they found it.

The meetings with B's birth mum also took place in secret and continued to be something she kept from her own children. Her children, however, weren't easily fooled, and despite not knowing (consciously) about their mother's history, they had picked up on key bits of information. On one of her visits to her birth mother, B took her children but didn't explain to them that the woman they were meeting was their grandmother. She was shocked when one of her children quickly pointed out a similarity between B and the "lady" they had come to meet, exclaiming "Look Mummy, you both have the same hands!"

I wondered what effect this continued need for hiding the truth had had on B: had this also been something that had led her into working with birth mothers and her need to get to the truth? She initially thought that she hadn't really questioned the deception, but, much later, she realized that she had also been hiding her desire and her healthy need to know and understand more. She thinks that this did play a part in motivating her to get alongside mothers who do not or cannot keep their babies. She also thinks that the not-knowing or keeping things hidden from even her adoptive parents had made it difficult for her to be authentic for so much of her life—something that affects the mothers she works with, who struggle to accept themselves and claim their histories.

She remembers that she had always been expected to show appreciation to her adoptive family "for taking in someone else's child", and how her siblings, who were the birth children of her adoptive parents, had reminded her repeatedly that she should be "grateful and good". They had also threatened that if she ever "misbehaved", she would be "sent back". B found this particularly confusing, as she didn't understand what being "sent back" meant and where she would be sent back to! She articulated how hard and upsetting this kind of communication can be for an adopted child who has not known or cannot remember any other life before being adopted, and how it prevents the expression of genuine emotion and the capacity to establish trusting relationships with others.

> "It's like you are always on your guard. I was living in limbo all those years, and being in limbo means you can't tell the truth and yet you don't want to tell lies."

Knowing that love was conditional was limiting for B, and she recognized how it had affected her relationships. However, she acknowledges that she had a strong constitution and resilience and therefore continued to want to understand why. She has started to think about her past as something she can continue to learn from and has used her experiences—even those she previously had no conscious memory of, like the loss of her birth mother—to help her in her work.

Together, we reflected on the complexity of attachments within every family but especially for adoptive families, where there have been fundamental losses for parents and children, losses that stir up primitive and conflicted feelings. Often, the experience of feeling conflicted or lost cannot be properly processed and therefore gets passed down through the generations. This makes it difficult to locate the original "carrier" of the "lost-child" identity. As B helpfully articulated, "knowing that you come from two different places, and being aware of how lost and also divided you feel, can be destabilizing or, at the very least, confusing".

It is hard enough for an adult to bear, but for a small child who has little opportunity to escape the confusion and conflict and is told not to question things, the result can be catastrophic. Many children turn their despair and confusion inwards, blaming themselves for being rejected. They may also be furious about it, finding any number of reasons why they shouldn't trust or risk reaching out to others. If the child grows up without the help and support needed to make sense of these experiences, then his or her internal conflicts and experiences of loss will be replicated or transferred to others.

Charles Dickens touches on the theme of secrets carried deep within each *human heart* and how difficult it is to truly know the other, in *A Tale of Two Cities* (1859):

A wonderful fact to reflect upon, that every human creature is constituted to be that profound secret and mystery to every other. A solemn consideration, when I enter a great city by night, that every one of those darkly clustered houses encloses its own secret; that every room in every one of them encloses its own secret; that every beating heart in the hundreds of thousands of breasts there, is, in some of its imaginings, a secret to the heart nearest it!

Throughout their lives, then, adopted individuals may well feel the powerful influences of both families. This makes it potentially harder for them to negotiate future separations and losses or to be truthful and open about what they feel and who they are. Bowlby (1973) describes what a baby or child who has not had a secure attachment with his or her mother/parent will feel about intimacy and separation:

[Y]earning and searching for the missing mother, sadness, increasing protest at her absence and growing anger with her for staying away, increased ambivalence on return home and evident fear of being separated again. [p. 41]

B emphasizes the importance of adoption support currently available through (some) social care teams, providing children, young people, and their parents with a life-line when times are really tough. This support is what is needed, she says, to help them make sense of the "yearning and searching". This is something that just wasn't available to her or her adoptive family: "So little was known or shared about birth parents, back then."

She wants the government to think long and hard about proposed cuts to adoption support services and what this would mean to struggling families and the young people who want to understand/access their histories or make contact with their birth families. She is also concerned that a lack of funding could also mean that birth mothers will not have access to the help they need in order to be able to contemplate their children's needs and feelings.

"Professionals trained and experienced enough to understand these complex issues can say the hard things that need to be said. They can help us with what we need to know."

B still feels a sadness for the child she once was, trying so hard to please and yet facing rejection on so many fronts. Understandably, she found aspects of family life painful and confusing, but she did not have anyone to turn to. She explains that despite her life being difficult at times, there were still precious and good experiences with her family, and she cared deeply for her adoptive parents. She argues that enforced adoptions are much more problematic, as they leave both child and birth parent feeling suddenly severed from each other and deeply distressed by this separation—an experience that, she says, will stay with them potentially for the rest of their lives.

"Parents who aren't able to keep their children but desperately want to need significant support to think about appropriate contact or preparing to let their children go."

In the case of the mother of Baby number 9, it will inevitably be a difficult journey, and she is yet to face the emotional pain (without employing all her avoidant strategies) of losing eight babies. The impact of these losses will no doubt be keenly felt at some stage, despite the delight of holding on to Baby number 9. B does not know how things will work out in the long term, but helping this mother and others like her to understand their behaviours and histories is key to facilitating meaningful change. It has also been a way of bringing B closer to mothers like her own birth mother, who relinquish or lose their babies.

B concludes our interview by acknowledging how meaningful it has been for her to contemplate her history without blaming herself for the rejections she has suffered. Her self-acceptance and recognition of her "inward treasure" has not only drawn her into valuable and fulfilling work, but has also kept her alive emotionally and enabled her to build healthy, loving relationships in her adult life.

CHAPTER NINE

Side by side: the importance of continuity of care

It was the best of times, it was the worst of times, it was the age of wisdom, it was the age of foolishness, it was the epoch of belief, it was the epoch of incredulity, it was the season of light, it was the season of darkness, it was the spring of hope, it was the winter of despair.

Charles Dickens, *A Tale of Two Cities* (1859)

Most of the adoption experiences and stories covered in this book describe a journey (as explored in chapter 4) or a process of transition and growth. Like so many aspects of life, especially those that centre around our interactions with others, this journey is not an easy one. It could, perhaps, be thought of as a quest full of challenges and risks, one in which the landscape may suddenly change. In the words of Dickens, "the spring of hope" could so easily transform into "the winter of despair".

Quests have been written about throughout ancient and modern literature, and they include trials and tribulations. One of the main objectives of a quest is to gain greater knowledge and understanding through the process of seeking and exploring, as described by Charlotte Brontë (1847) in *Jane Eyre*:

I remembered that the real world was wide, and that a varied field of hopes and fears, of sensations and excitements, awaited those who had the courage to go forth into its expanse, to seek real knowledge of life amidst its perils. [Charlotte Brontë, *Jane Eyre*]

Some quests may also be lonely and confusing and will require considerable resolve and internal resources to make it through the times of isolation. As the poem at the end of chapter 4 shows, the adoption experience will have its ups and downs, with moments of pure joy as well times of despair. However, the fact that there can be such shifts or fluctuations in the landscape of the adoption experience, and in a relatively short space of time, also creates a dilemma for professionals.

Parents have described to me how they go through "seasons" when their need is great but also immediate, whereas at other happier or sunnier times there may not be a specific role for professionals. This does not mean that all interventions should suddenly come to end, but unfortunately the way many services are set up and managed is that resources are available only during a time of crisis. There are those families who "bounce" from one crisis to another with very little space in between, and professionals remain engaged with them; however, there are also plenty of other families who say that they lose touch in the "better" times and then have to endure a lengthy wait when they need to re-engage. Parents also describe an experience of being re-referred to a service where they had previously been known and had felt understood, only to discover that the "familiar" and trusted professionals have left or have moved to another team.

This chapter, then, is about the importance of continuity of care, something that parents say they most appreciate from services. I think this is because establishing a relationship with a professional who then leaves can be destabilizing for a family, whereas a commitment to providing continuity for families helps to prevent the experience of loss being replicated. Having a consistent presence from one or two professionals who can hold on to the different narratives for the family can also help parents to regulate what McDougall (1978) refers to as "primitive communications". It is these primitive and preverbal or "hard to put into words" feelings that seem to cause the most upset within the family dynamic and therefore require careful and reflective attention. If regulation can be achieved, even if the behaviours do not change, then a deeper level of trust and confidence between the family and professionals can be achieved.

"I didn't really see why we as parents were being advised to get help—as a couple. It was A who needed therapy, not us. . . . So we were frustrated when [our social worker] suggested we join the parenting group. . . . We also trusted her, because she has known our family for a long time and we have learned so much from her . . ."

It is also clear from available evidence that investing in vulnerable individuals through providing continuity in their relationships with trusted professionals has specific health benefits and even improves mortality rates. Research by the University of Exeter's Medical School analysed 22 studies, examining the relationship between continuity of care and death rates. The conclusion was that, in 18 out of the 22 studies (82%), having contact with the same doctor over time resulted in "significantly fewer deaths" among patients.

Professor Philip Evans, of the University of Exeter Medical School, emphasized that "continuity of care" helps doctor and patient "get to know each other", and that this has many obvious benefits, including better communications. He also described how, in recent times, "the human aspect" of general practice has been "neglected". Sir Denis Pereira Gray, a GP who collaborated on the Exeter study, described continuity of care as being "a matter of life and death" (Pereira Gray, Sidaway-Lee, White, Thorne, & Evans, 2018).

Investing in families for the longer term can, therefore, actually improve their relationships and life chances, while also saving the state time and money. This happens when professionals know their families well enough to be able to intercept and prevent a crisis or, at the very least, provide them with a "safety harness" to minimize the risk during these times.

"There's no substitute for building good relationships and working your differences out through taking time and listening. Everyone's looking for the quick fix, but that's not how life is lived or love is loved. It's more complicated than that . . ."

(Adoptive parents of adolescents)

My own experience, backed up by Selwyn, Wijedasa, and Meakings (2014), and also explored in chapter 4, shows that many adoptive parents feel that they have been forgotten about or abandoned by professionals, and they also feel ostracized by and excluded from their local community.

"My son never understood why he wasn't invited to birthday parties— even when the rest of the class were included. It destroyed us to see parents who we thought were our friends making it clear to us that we weren't wanted, and we would never be on their 'A-list' (or their B-list, for that matter). People just didn't want to make the effort, once they saw how challenging our son was and how hard things were for us at home."

(Parents of an adopted child with an ADHD diagnosis)

Most of the parents discussed in this book expressed how they felt "unprepared" for their adoption journey with their "new" children. This was also the case for those who were very positive about the involvement and support they received later on. Introductions were described as uncomfortable or "awkward", and many parents also felt ill-prepared for taking on a child with complex needs. These parents each have their own accounts of what felt like a lengthy and gruelling process of assessment, but then, as soon as a baby or child had been identified for them, the final and very important stage of the process was "rushed" through. This gave them and their adopted child little time to adapt or prepare for the huge changes they would all face.

Some reflected on the shock of having to get to know a child in as little as five days, with no chance to meet them first and explore their own doubts or anxieties. I have not referred to overseas adoptions here, but my understanding is that these adoptions can also happen quickly and that the child has little time to prepare for such a change. This early stage of the adoption process—the beginning of a new journey together—was therefore described by parents as being "distressing" or "traumatic", and I could see how it had stirred up powerful and primitive feelings that had made a lasting impression on them.

> "We were shown a photo and asked what we felt about this strange child—just from their photo! We had no idea what to expect, but we felt under pressure to say we felt love for someone we didn't know and hadn't even met."

When a child is placed for adoption, other family members and friends are encouraged to stay away, in order to help the child have a settling-in period. However, for some adopters this situation sets up an early sense of isolation in that they cannot celebrate the arrival of a child with their loved ones in the normal way.

I am confident that there are good reasons for this, such as to allow the child and parents to get to know each other and for the child to adapt to a new environment without too many comings and goings of others. However, I do wonder if this (in the early weeks and months) is where the extended "professional family" could have a role in being more available to the adoptive family.

With a new baby, there is usually a midwife and then a health visitor who has regular contact with the family and who will check that the baby is feeding, sleeping, and so forth (although this situation has changed recently through lack of resources). Getting the right support (or the support right) at the start for adoptive families is something that seems to come up time and time again for parents. This early-intervention approach to supporting a child placed with a new family is more likely to happen for children and young people in the care system, but it is not routinely available for adopted children and their parents. Perhaps this is why adopters feel that once the adoption order has been granted, they are generally left to "get on with it".

In his book *Nurturing Natures; Attachment and Children's Emotional, Sociocultural and Brain Development* (2017), Graham Music draws from research that points to "maternal commitment" as being the best predictor for infant survival. However, the survival rates are highest (and the children are healthier) when there is a strong community and family network around a child—particularly one that includes the maternal grandmother (Kramer, 2015). Adopted children have not had the maternal attentiveness and protectiveness that they needed to survive and thrive. This leaves me wondering why there is no statutory provision available to new adoptive parents or a "professional parent" or "grandparent" who would keep a protective "eye" on the new parents and their baby.

I am aware that in this chapter I am focusing on continuity, which advocates for a longer period of involvement and potentially the provision of more resources, at a time when "the purse is empty", as one manager put it. However, from my experience it is this experience of neglect and abandonment that creates the most problems for families and generates a greater need for resources further down the line.

The merits of early intervention are known about and well researched, and yet too often within the public sector we go for the short-term gain; we continue to neglect those who are in great need and only act when there is a crisis. Surely it would be better use of scarce resources to provide a low-level but consistent presence at the start of the journey?

I have recently wondered about the merits of establishing a version of an antenatal group for approved adopters before they begin their adoption journey with their children in earnest—a group where they would at least have the ongoing contact and support of other parents going through similar experiences.

"Just knowing that someone was there who understood our family made us feel so much better somehow. In your last call, when you didn't really do anything . . . you were just there listening . . . I realized I could carry on . . ."
(Adoptive parent of two adolescents)

Defining when a family is in crisis and requires urgent help is complicated, but professionals who know the family well can pick up on significant changes in the state of mind of the referred child or young person and how the family functions in relation to an increased risk. These changes may be happening in the environment, but they might also be linked to key relationships. For example, the level of disturbance can escalate when an already traumatized individual comes into contact with the distress of another. I find that in some cases a crisis can be connected to a loss or increased stress for a parent, such as facing the illness or death of one of their parents or encountering major difficulties at work (possibly taking us back again to the "still face" of the caregiver). If communications about distress cannot be heard or contained within families, then the situation becomes amplified, and the feelings can become intolerable. This situation feels frantic for all involved, and tensions will escalate without intervention.

Over the years of working with adoption, I have seen the difference that working *side by side* with professionals can make for struggling adoptive families. It makes perfect sense that they would fare so much better than those who do not have access to anywhere near the level of support they need in order to be able to function as a family, or those who, for whatever reason, choose to isolate themselves.

This approach is especially important for families with children who have been severely traumatized or compromised very early on in their lives. With these children it is not only important but essential that interventions and close working relationships are established as early as possible between all those who are central in a child's life (see Health and Social Care Committee, 2019).

Untreated trauma has a way of working its way into the heart of every system so that it can be clearly felt. I have been in meetings with professionals who can all articulate their understanding of splitting (Klein, 1932) and containment (Bion, 1967), but when splitting begins to happen in the network, there are always some who will respond defensively if this is pointed out. I have lost count of how many times there will be at least one professional who claims that he or she alone can represent the true needs or perspectives of the child or young person. The fear of having to face the trauma within the child can, therefore, unfortunately, prevent professionals from being able to challenge and contain the anxiety that so easily gets into the system and impedes the capacity to work collaboratively with families.

Another area of trauma that even we as mental health practitioners are still learning about is how adverse conditions in the womb can affect the developing baby. There is more understanding and research available about what happens when the foetus is regularly exposed to negative influences in the womb. Foetal alcohol spectrum disorder is a term used to describe a whole range of life-affecting difficulties and disabilities that can be caused through a woman using alcohol during the course of her pregnancy. Alcohol affects developing cells in the baby and disrupts the mitochondrial system, which is responsible for energy production and normal development (Mather, 2018). As a disorder, FASD is now understood to be far more complex than when it was first studied in the 1970s. The damage can be especially severe to the baby's brain and spinal cord, potentially leaving a child who has been compromised in this way with limited executive functioning. In other words, it affects memory and the capacity to process certain information. It may also diminish the ability to empathize and regulate emotions, making it very difficult for an individual affected to show a genuine desire to interact with others. These kinds of problems are, unfortunately, becoming more common for the adopted cohort of children and young people in our society, and it is important therefore to acknowledge that even the most nurturing and consistent adoptive parents will struggle to manage these kinds of complex presentations and behaviours on their own.

"The world expects things of my son. Expectations he is not capable of fulfilling."

(Parent of a child with an FASD diagnosis)

Even those well-resourced parents who come from close-knit families or communities say that they came to realize quite soon into the adoption how different they were from the child they had adopted, and how difficult it was, therefore, to reach them (Kenrick, Lindsey, & Tollemache, 2006). John Simmonds (2008) describes how an adopted child can create or bring with him to his new family "an emotional atmosphere that is profoundly disturbing" and how the parents' "reasonable assumption" that they will develop a greater understanding of their child's needs can be sorely challenged over time. Many parents will sooner or later recognize that they do not have the resources on their own to continue to adapt to the changing and challenging presentations of their children.

At every significant stage of this child's life, the parent will need to access some support, insight, and understanding, from the early years into school and beyond. Unfortunately, a large number of schools exclude children and young people who exhibit challenging behaviours, and there is little training and support available in schools to build awareness around these kinds of issues relating to early life traumas and difficulties. At the time of writing, it is also a fairly recent development for adopted children with specific and potentially complex needs to be given the additional support they need. Previously only children identified as being in the care system were given additional support and preferential treatment regarding school placements and access to mental health services. The added complication relating to adopted children is that they do not always stand out as having noticeable difficulties in settings like school, because they have learned how to "merge" into the background or to dissociate to protect themselves from further exposure, humiliation, or harm.

Over the years of working with children and adolescents in mental health services and, before that, in art and youth projects, I have witnessed how children who are repeatedly threatened, neglected, or exploited can "give up" if left to struggle alone. This is the point where intervention is essential before something changes for the child and any desire he or she has to invest in human society is lost. These children and adolescents can become the most challenging individuals to work with, and they are more likely to develop ingrained antisocial behaviours and attitudes. One young person explained to me that she reached a point where she "forgot" to care and would do almost anything to avoid "having a feeling" or being emotionally close to others.

The portrait I have painted of adoption might seem rather dark and very much overshadowed by loss, which may have come as a shock to those with little experience of adoption: by the time families arrive at the front door of specialist adoption or mental health services, they are confused and potentially traumatized by what they have experienced. They also, understandably, want to communicate their urgent need for services to "fix" what is "broken" in their family. However, once they feel that they have been heard and understood, they generally do become more interested in finding meaning and genuinely want someone to shed light on their situation.

"I just want someone to tell me why he behaves like this, what he is saying to us, and what we should be doing to help him."

The child or young person also (usually) knows that he or she is causing some distress and that it doesn't feel very comfortable living in such a negative environment. The young person can therefore experience genuine relief when an experienced and insightful practitioner recognizes the need to "gather up" and integrate split-off or hidden aspects of the family and the family's story without rushing for an immediate "solution". By containing and taking in a "truer" version of events over time, the practitioner (therapist or social worker) can draw the focus away from the crisis without avoiding the pain. This approach of working in little areas of light to illuminate the richness hiding within the shadows reminds me of the way the artist Rembrandt [1606–1669] painted his portraits.

This approach also fits with Anne Alvarez's concept of bringing "live company" to the traumatized child (1992); with Bion's insistence on engaging with projections in the therapeutic relationship (projective identification; 1967); and van der Kolk's emphasis on establishing safety and trust before the therapist can get underneath the protective, dissociative defence and reach the "Self that is confident, curious, and calm" (2014).

An adopter once instructed me to "keep it real" in my work with him and his family, and he appreciated the bold and challenging conversations we were having. It had taken us some time to get to a point where he could recognize that he had been projecting unwanted aspects of himself and his adoption experience into me—such was his fear of failure and his sense of shame and inadequacy at not being able to "undo" what could not be "undone" for his adopted children. He and his partner had found some relief in the "fight" and in my challenging their wish to hide rather than face the difficulties. In the words of Herodotus, in his *Histories* (c. 425 BC),

> It is better by noble boldness to run the risk of being subject to half of the evils we anticipate than to remain in cowardly listlessness for fear of what might happen.

Based on feedback and on my experience of working with families over the years, I would argue that there could be a number of improved outcomes to having a more side-by-side approach to adoption support. Every story has the potential for change, where the narrative takes us down a different path from the one we were expecting—like those interactive novels, where readers can influence the ending through the decisions they make as they read the book. I have witnessed how even some of the most distressing symptoms related to early life traumas can diminish when there has been at least someone who has provided insightful and alive "company" for a good part of the journey.

This is where the light really enters the frame, for I have encountered numerous children and young people who have had very troubling and traumatic starts to their lives, but who continue to be creative, resourceful, and resilient. What is interesting is that each of them can provide an account of having experienced at least one "good" relationship at key points in their lives where they had received encouragement and nurture.

There are a number of longitudinal attachment studies to back up this hypothesis. A child who has a secure attachment to at least one parent figure will be more likely to go on to form good and reciprocal friendships (Groh et. al., 2014, cited in Music, 2017; Sroufe, 2005). In the case of adopted children and young people, some of them have received this from a foster carer or from a relative from the extended family. Others describe having had a consistent relationship with a "trusted" professional, such as a teacher, therapist, or social worker:

"When I lost my phone, I panicked. My social worker, who has known me pretty much all my life, is the only who still calls me . . . she doesn't seem to care that people don't really do phone calls anymore."

(Young person, age 17 years)

What is inspiring is that these children and young people have learned to take what they can from the little bit of soil and light they have been given, so that the shoot continues to grow. As professionals—often working in stretched services—we cannot ever hope to compensate them for all the loss that they have experienced or totally wipe out the deficit. We can, however, positively influence a child's life through building or enabling others to build consistent relationships that can provide the continuity and nurture required to help redress the balance.

Conclusions: "It's been emotional"

> Life, although it may only be an accumulation of anguish, is dear to me, and I will defend it.
>
> Mary Wolstonecraft Shelley, *Frankenstien* (1818)

Iarrive at the end of this book with a keen sense of responsibility to all those who have entrusted their adoption stories to me. I want to make sure that their key messages do not get lost, watered down, or distorted, but within the "tell it how it really is" plea lies a challenge: how can I focus on the positives without denying the despair and anguish in these stories while maintaining a sense of balance?

In chapter 9, I used the analogy of illuminating the richness hiding within the shadows of a painting, creating a juxtaposition between light and darkness, so that more hopeful feelings can enter the frame. It feels fitting, then, that I am introducing "hope" or hopefulness as the final touches are being applied. This is because, in my experience, important details relating to an emotional or complicated situation do not emerge until the ending is in sight. This happens frequently in psychotherapy sessions, where a significant or profound piece of information is shared just as the session is concluding. Perhaps it is the imminent ending itself that makes this possible, but it is a scenario I can relate to.

When I worked as an artist (years ago), it was usual for me to set about changing a small but important detail in a painting that had long since been "completed"—a detail I hadn't been aware of while I was immersed in the primary process of "making" or painting. There are a number of reasons why this happens, but it is not necessarily about avoidance.

I have had the same experience in trying to bring this book to an end, in that I have completed and then deleted various versions of the ending because they felt too hopeful or "glossy". Fortunately, I realized that I had overlooked a small but very important detail that makes both perspectives possible. It is a detail that is hard to quantify, because it is about the complex emotional process of relating to others and the "magic" ingredient or catalyst leading to meaningful change. Much has been written about the importance of a positive therapeutic alliance and how this is the most effective aspect of treatment, regardless of the modality, but Allan Schore articulates this view further. He argues that a more intuitive or instinctive way of relating to one another comes from the right hemisphere of the brain (2000) and that our emotional processes lie at the foundation of a model of instinctive behaviour. This means that these "right-brain to right-brain" interactions are the ones that create the strongest emotional connections or bonds.

Schore draws on the work of Bowlby, the father of attachment theory (1958, 1969), who combined Darwin's theories about evolution and biology with Freud's discoveries in psychoanalysis to show how attachment is instinctive behaviour with a biological function (Schore, 2000). These "instinctive" interactions are vital for healthy development in that they help to establish secure early attachments, but they also remain central to the process of relating to others throughout our lives. This is because they help to regulate (or manage) our powerful feelings, including those that relate to our infantile experiences (Schore, 2000, 2012).

In chapter 4, I wrote about the significance of "meaningful attachments" for the baby, and how disruptions and separations negatively affect the parent–infant relationship. An adopted child who has been separated from his or her birth parents is unlikely to have had the opportunity to develop a *meaningful attachment*—that is, an instinctive emotional and physical attachment—with his or her birth parent(s). It is this primary "absence" that can, unfortunately, become one of the main areas of difficulty for a child who feels deeply affected by this primary deprivation.

As professionals or parents, we are usually able to recognize the significance of this loss on an emotional level, and we may also be able to think about how to address the physical deficits through providing good care. However, combining both the physical and emotional nurture "instinctively" is something many adoptive parents and professionals supporting them, find hugely challenging. Some parents tell me that they "get" their child emotionally but really struggle to manage the physical expressions of emotion, such as screaming, running away, overeating, hitting out, smearing or wetting, and so on. Others, on the other hand, describe being able to meet the physical demands of their child through providing good physical care when it can be received and through regularly clearing up all kinds of physical mess. They do, however, admit to finding it very difficult to forge and maintain an emotional connectivity with their child.

It is a big ask for a parent to "practise" this unique combination of emotional and physical responses and to be intuitive and sensitive to every fluctuating state of mind, especially given that the "blueprint" for "right-brain to right-brain" interactions has not been forged in early infancy. Aristotle's "the whole is greater than the sum of its parts" perhaps also applies here, for it would be oversimplifying things to say that the most rewarding and life-affirming human interactions are merely a combination of emotional and biological responses.

Perhaps this fundamental loss at the start of life is at least one of the main reasons why endings inevitably stir up such complex feelings for adopted children and young people. Endings are a painful reminder of traumatic beginnings, where the infant or young child was not able to access a "regulatory system" (Schore, 2000) and where the instinctive right-brain-focused attempts to connect were not reciprocated or were painfully rejected. An infant in this predicament would have felt overwhelmed by unregulated feelings and may have associated being parented with memories (conscious or unconscious) of being *lost* rather than of feeling *found* and loved.

In chapter 1, I used the analogy of a garden to illustrate how a child can "come to life" if he or she is noticed and nurtured "in time", before the weeds or brambles of prolonged trauma have had the chance to suffocate or stifle necessary growth. Frances Hodgson Burnett's story, *The Secret Garden*, articulates this perfectly, revealing how the emotional and physical aspects of a child called Mary begin to come together and work instinctively to bring the garden (and herself) to life. This is only possible when Mary begins to feel understood and "at home" in the natural world, for, despite her "sour" nature, she is becoming curious about life and therefore desires the company of others. She is well attended to by one of the maids, Martha, but, more importantly, she is also watched over by the mother of Dickon, Susan Sowerby. This mother figure, who is also connected to the natural world, is a "sower" of good seeds and the one who provides a regulatory function for Mary—the antidote for her "sourness". She is also the one who recognizes that Mary needs emotional and physical nurture, and so she supplies "rich new milk with cream on the top of it . . . and cottage-made currant buns". But she also provides physical resources, like a skipping rope, and she intercedes for Mary to have her own "bit of earth . . . to plant seeds in—to make things grow—to see them come alive".

I recall a child who brought to his therapy session a bean that he had planted. It had shot up and appeared to be healthy and was growing well, despite being in a plastic cup and having only a small amount of soil. I had the impression that he was pleased that he had played a part in bringing something to life, but he was also confused. He wanted me to explain to him what had made the bean grow, asking: "how come this [the shoot] is bigger than the bean?"

I tried to explain that the bean shoot had a root that was taking its food from the soil, and that the shoot also took nurture from the sunlight. These, together with what was already inside the bean, made it grow. He looked at the little bit of soil with some dismay and then declared that he thought that there must also be "a little bit of magic" helping the bean to "grow out". There was something very reassuring for him about the certainty that a thing that is alive, with just a bit of good soil, will always be on the move. However, his concern that the nurture or good soil might run out was also evident. This was a communication about his own early experiences of having had an affectionate beginning with his birth mother, who, unfortunately, due to her addictions, could not maintain the growth. The "good soil" did, therefore, effectively run out. However, this profound comment and childish wisdom stayed with me and was perhaps one of the prompts I needed to re-read *The Secret Garden*.

Schore (2000) explains this in relation to a human infant and how the early social environment interacts with the maturing organism in order to shape developmental processes. We can quantify what we mean by "a little bit of magic" within "developmental processes" in psychoanalytic terms: for example, reverie, alpha functioning, and containment (Bion, 1962b); emotional holding (Winnicott, 1953, 1960); a secure attachment (Bowlby, 1969); the regulating of projective processes (Klein, 1937, 1946; Schore, 2000); developing a sense of self (Stern, 1985); and the capacity to mentalize or mentalization (Fonagy et. al., 1998, 2006). Bion also came up with a further understanding of the significance of the mother's role in the early social environment—which is to develop the child's "mental apparatus" (1962b, 1967). Without her regulating presence and attentive interaction, the infant or child (the maturing organism) will grow with a skewed view of the world.

The adoptive parents' role is, therefore, more significant than over-seeing the organic growth of the child, as they will have to work harder to prepare the soil, which has become dried out and depleted through lack of nurture and has been contaminated by loss or trauma. The professional working closely with the adoptive family should therefore have a role in overseeing the interactions between children or adolescents and their parents and in helping parents to develop the "mental apparatus" required for such a daunting task. The professional may also need to fulfil a number of other roles, such as that of a midwife or health visitor, but at times they could, perhaps, think of themselves of being like a psychological "gardener" tending to the "soil" that provides the emotional nurture while regulating the extremes in the environment. When this can be achieved, it becomes possible for the struggling "organism" to maintain a steady growth.

This is a rather optimistic picture, admittedly, and I am back to using metaphors and analogies to describe what in reality can feel far away from the beautiful imagery of a healthy garden. But what I understand from gardeners is that while the process of keeping a garden thriving can be "magical", it is also backbreaking and relentless. I asked a keen gardener who is restoring a large, old garden to its former glory to describe the process:

"You feel like you can't take your eyes off it and you have to keep on top of things. You therefore have to keep working at it, but you also have to know when to give it the chance to grow without too much meddling. But there are wonderful times and many surprises . . ."

In the parent groups I have facilitated over the years of being in a specialist adoption service, I have observed each group entering a phase or stage where parents begin to feel safe enough to be honest about how tough it really is for them. They begin to talk openly about the pressure (and exhaustion) of always having to keep on top of things. They are aware that the difficulties they are facing as a family are chronic and that these are not suddenly going to be resolved. However, I have also noticed how the anger subsides when we can think about how these difficulties might be better contained or regulated and how the healthy aspects of the family can be protected. Despite everything, parents can begin to acknowledge that there is evidence of growth.

One parent admitted that she was beginning to learn "what I should be doing and feeling" and that this learning through the regulating presence of the facilitators had enabled her to "work out the 'doing' bit". As the group progressed, she acknowledged that what she had appreciated most over the course of the group was being part of a "community" where others understood and validated her experiences. In one session she announced: "I'm starting to understand that you have to fake it to make it sometimes and that it's ok to do that!"

She had been relieved to find that "instinctive" parenting hadn't happened automatically for other parents either and that it had had to be practised. This appears to be a contradictory statement in that "instinctive" would seem to imply that something happens "naturally".

This brings us back to the beginning and to how, when we choose to learn through our observations and experience, we can begin to develop the mental capacity or "apparatus" to respond instinctively (Bion, 1967). This process has also been summarized by Broadwell (1969) for the world of work as a "competence cycle". He described this process as "the four levels of teaching".

1. Unconscious incompetence.

2. Conscious incompetence.

3. Conscious competence.

4. Unconscious competence.

This model has been adapted and re-branded through various diagrams and charts for numerous organizations, but it would appear that instinctive behaviour, or the unconscious competent way of operating and relating, is the ultimate aim for successful living and productivity in the workplace.

This view challenges the dominant focus on therapeutic approaches working specifically with the conscious mind. They are generally short-term approaches (such as cognitive behavioural therapy, CBT) that can help the referred individual become more *consciously competent* in managing his or her difficulties. These approaches are also relatively easy to measure in terms of effectiveness. For those who are suffering from the effects of developmental trauma and relational difficulties rooted in infancy, I would argue that there is a need for a more instinctive and relational approach to treatment, an approach that acknowledges the existence of the unconscious.

This is not necessarily going to be a comfortable message, and I hope that by highlighting the challenges in this way I have drawn attention to the need for continued provision of multiple and specialist resources. I write this at a time of political and social change where there is heightened anxiety and austerity. Whole teams and services are being dismantled and have lost large amounts of central government funding. This predicament is having far-reaching implications for local communities and those groups of people in society who are most vulnerable (especially children). But, ultimately, this state of affairs affects everyone and limits our capacity to be hopeful and creative. This is the bigger picture, where commissioners, leaders, and politicians appear to have "forgotten" that relationships matter and that getting it right from the beginning of a life is vital for the health of society and the economy.

To conclude, I give you this little book about adoption, which has become rather like a group portrait, with representatives from different generations, birth families, and adoptive families and with the creative couple at the centre. There are layers upon layers of relationships, some hiding in the shadows. The dynamics of such a group cannot possibly be understood through one brief viewing, but it is set within the natural landscape of the garden where growth and change is possible.

I sincerely hope, therefore, that it will serve as a reminder to those driving our obsession with quick fixes and performance management, that investing in relationships can save lives and, indeed, money. For when we can be helped to develop instinctive and meaningful connections with others, we can truly begin to address the deficits.

REFERENCES

Adamson, L., & Frick, J. (2003). The still face: A history of a shared experimental paradigm. *Infancy, 4* (4): 451–473.

Ainsworth, M. D. S. (1968). Object relations, dependency, and attachment: A theoretical review of the infant–mother relationship. *Child Development, 40*: 969–1025.

Ainsworth, M. D. S., Blehar, M. C., Waters, E., & Wall, S. (1978). *Patterns of Attachment: A Psychological Study of the Strange Situation*. Hillsdale, NJ: Lawrence Erlbaum.

Alvarez, A. (1992). *Live Company*. London: Tavistock/Routledge.

Balint, M. (1968). *The Basic Fault: Therapeutic Aspects of Regression*. London: Tavistock Publications. Reprinted New York: Brunner/Mazel, 1979.

Barratt, S., & Lobatto, W. (2016). *Surviving and Thriving in Care and Beyond: Personal and Professional Perspectives*. London: Karnac.

Barrie, J. M. (1863). *Peter Pan*. Bristol: Parragon, 1998.

Bateman, A., & Fonagy, P. (2004). *Psychotherapy for Borderline Personality Disorder: Mentalization Based Treatment*. Oxford: Oxford University Press.

Beebe, B. (2006). Co-constructing mother–infant distress in face-to-face interactions: Contributions of microanalysis. *Infant Observation, 9* (2): 151–164.

Beebe, B., & Lachman, F. (2002). *Infant Research and Adult Treatment*. Hillsdale, NJ: Analytic Press.

Beebe, N. (2014). My journey in infant research and psychoanalysis: Microanalysis, a social microscope. *Psychoanalytic Psychology, 31*: 4–25.

Bion, W. R. (1959). Attacks on linking. *International Journal of Psychoanalysis, 40* (5–6): 308–315.

Bion, W. R. (1961). *Experiences in Groups and Other Papers*. London: Tavistock.

Bion, W. R. (1962a). The psychoanalytic study of thinking. *International Journal of Psychoanalysis, 43* (4–5). Reprinted as "A theory of thinking" in: *Second Thoughts: Selected Papers on Psychoanalysis* (pp. 110–119). London: Heinemann, 1967; London: Karnac, 1984.

Bion, W. R. (1962b). *Learning from Experience*. London: Heinemann. Reprinted London: Karnac, 1984.

Bion, W. R. (1967). *Second Thoughts: Selected Papers on Psychoanalysis*. London: Heinemann. Reprinted London: Karnac, 1984.

Bion, W. R. (1970). *Attention and Interpretation*. London: Tavistock. Reprinted London: Karnac, 1984.

Bion, W. R. (1987). *Clinical Seminars and Other Works*. London: Karnac, 2000.

Blos, P. (1991). Sadomasochism and the defence against recall of painful affect. *Journal of the American Psychoanalytic Association, 39* (2): 417–429.

Bower, M. (2005). *Psychoanalytic Theory for Social Work Practice: Thinking Under Fire*. London: Routledge.

Bower, M., & Solomon, R. (2018). *What Social Workers Need to Know: A Psychoanalytic Approach*. London: Routledge.

Bowlby, J. (1958). The nature of the child's tie to his mother. *International Journal of Psychoanalysis, 39*: 1–23.

Bowlby, J. (1969). *Attachment and Loss, Vol. 1. Attachment*. New York: Basic Books.

Bowlby, J. (1973). *Attachment and Loss, Vol. 2. Separation: Anxiety and Anger*. New York: Basic Books.

Bowlby, J. (1980). *Attachment and Loss, Vol. 3. Loss: Sadness and Depression*. London: Hogarth Press.

Britton, R. J. (1981). Re-enactment as an unwitting professional response to family dynamics. In: S. Box, B. Copley, J. Magagna, & E. Moustaki (Eds.), *Psychotherapy with Families: An Analytic Approach* (pp. 48–58). London: Routledge.

Britton, R. (1998). *Belief and Imagination*. London: Routledge.

Britton, R. (2003). Narcissistic problems in sharing space. In: *Sex, Death, and the Superego: Experiences in Psychoanalysis* (pp. 165–178). London: Karnac.

Broadwell, M. M. (1969). Teaching for learning (XVI). *The Gospel Guardian* (May, 2018). Available at: http://wordsfitlyspoken.org/gospel_guardian/v20/v20n41p1-3a.html

Brontë, C. (1847). *Jane Eyre*. London: Penguin Classics, 1985.

Busch, F. (Ed.) (2008). *Mentalization: Theoretical Considerations, Research Findings, and Clinical Implications*. New York: Routledge.

Carpy, D. V. (1989). Tolerating the countertransference: A mutative process. *International Journal of Psychoanalysis, 70* (2): 287–294.

Cicchetti, D., & Valentino, K. (2015). An ecological-transactional perspective on child maltreatment: Failure of the average expectable environment and its influence on child development. In: D. Cicchetti & D. Cohen

(Eds.), *Developmental Psychopathology, Vol. 3: Risk, Disorder, and Adaptation* (2nd ed., pp. 129–201). Hoboken, NJ: Wiley.

Cleavely, E. (1993). Relationships: Interaction, defences, and transformation. In: S. Ruszczynski (Ed.), *Psychotherapy with Couples*. London: Karnac.

Conway, P. (2009). Falling between minds: The effects of unbearable experiences on multi-agency communication in the care system. *Adoption & Fostering, 33* (1): 18–29.

Cooper, A., & Redfern, S. (2016). *Reflective Parenting: A Guide to Understanding What's Going on in Your Child's Mind*. London: Routledge.

Dickens, C. (1859). *A Tale of Two Cities*. London: Penguin Classics, 2003.

Dicks, H. V. (1967). *Marital Tensions: Clinical Studies Towards a Psychological Theory of Interaction*. London: Routledge & Kegan Paul.

Douet, V., Chang, L., Cloak, C., & Ernst, T. (2013). Genetic influences on brain developmental trajectories on neuro-imaging studies: From infancy to young adulthood. *Brain Imaging and Behavior, 8* (2014, No. 2): 234–250.

Emanuel, L. (2002). Deprivation × three: The contribution of organizational dynamics to the "triple deprivation" of looked-after children. *Journal of Child Psychotherapy, 28* (2): 163–179.

Feats, J., & Dibben, E. (2017). *What Social Workers Need to Know about Social Media and Adoption* [Video]. CoramBAAF Briefing Paper. London: Community Care Inform. Available at: www.communitycare. co.uk/2017/05/30/video-social-workers-need-know-social-media-adoption

Fonagy, P. (2002). *Affect Regulation, Mentalization, and the Development of the Self*. New York: Other Press.

Fonagy, P., Steele, H., & Steele, M. (1991). Maternal representations of attachment during pregnancy predict the organization of infant–mother attachment at one year of age. *Child Development, 62*: 891–905.

Fonagy, P., Target, M., Steele, H., & Steele, M. (1998). *Reflective Functioning Manual V5 for Application to Adult Attachment Interviews*. Psychoanalysis Unit, Department of Clinical Health Psychology, University of London.

Freud, A. (1958). Adolescence. *Psychoanalytic Study of the Child, 1* (13): 255–278.

Freud, S. (1895d) (with Breuer, J.). *Studies on Hysteria. Standard Edition, 2*.

Freud, S. (1905d). *Three Essays on the Theory of Sexuality. Standard Edition, 7*.

Freud, S. (1910d). The future prospects of psycho-analytic therapy. *Standard Edition, 11*.

Freud, S. (1915e). *The unconscious. Standard Edition, 14*.

Freud, S. (1924e). The loss of reality in neurosis and psychosis. *Standard Edition, 19*.

Grimm, J., & Grimm, W. (1812). *The Grimms' Fairy Tales [Kinder und Hausmärchen* (Children's and Household Tales)]. New York: Doubleday, 1977.

Groh, A. M., Fearon, R. P., Bakermans-Kranenburg, M. J., van Ijzendoorn, M. H., Steele, R. D., & Roisman, G. I. (2014). The significance of attachment security for children's social competence with peers: A meta-analytic study. *Attachment and Human Development, 16* (2): 103–136.

Harris, P. (2006). *In Search of Belonging.* London: British Association for Adoption and Fostering.

Harris, P. (2012). *Chosen: Living with Adoption.* London: British Association for Adoption and Fostering.

Health and Social Care Committee. (2019). *First 1000 Days of Life.* London: House of Commons. Available at: https://publications.parliament.uk/pa/cm201719/cmselect/cmhealth/1496/1496.pdf

Henry, G. (1974). Doubly deprived. *Journal of Child Psychotherapy, 3* (4): 15–28.

Hindle, D., & Shulman, G. (2008). *The Emotional Experience of Adoption: A Psychoanalytic Perspective.* London: Routledge.

Hinshelwood, R. D. (1994). Attacks on the reflective space. In: V. Schermer & M. Pines (Eds.), *Ring of Fire.* London: Routledge.

Hinshelwood, R. D. (2016). Couples and primitive processes. In: A. Novakovic (Ed.), *Couple Dynamics: Psychoanalytic Perspectives in Work with the Individual, the Couple, and the Group.* London: Karnac.

Hodges, J., Hillman, S., & Steele, M. (2007). *Story Stem Assessment Profile: Coding Manual and Protocol.* London: Anna Freud Centre.

Hodges, J., Steele, M., Hillman, S., Henderson, K., & Kaniuk, J. (2005). Change and continuity in mental representations of attachment after adoption. In: D. M. Brodzinsky & J. Palacios (Eds.), *Psychological Issues in Adoption* (pp. 93–116). Westport, CT: Praeger.

Hodgson Burnett, F. (1911). *The Secret Garden.* London: Heinemann. Reprinted London: Puffin, 1951.

Howe, D., Feast, J., & Coster, D. (2003). *Adoption, Search and Reunion: The Long-Term Experience of Adopted Adults.* London: British Association for Adoption and Fostering.

Howe, D., Sawbridge, P., & Hinings, D. (1992). *Half a Million Women: Mothers Who Lose Their Children by Adoption.* London: Penguin.

Hughes, D. (2011). *Attachment-Focused Family Therapy Workbook.* New York: Norton.

Iqbal, N. (2018). Generation Z: "We have more to do than drink and take drugs". *The Guardian,* 21 July. Available at: www.theguardian.com/society/2018/jul/21/generation-z-has-different-attitudes-says-a-new-report

Jaques, E. (1955). Social systems as a defence against persecutory and depressive anxiety. In: M. Klein, P. Heimann, & R. E. Money-Kyrle (Eds.), *New Directions in Psycho-Analysis.* London: Tavistock Publications. Reprinted London: Karnac, 1985.

Joseph, B. (1982). Addiction to near death. *International Journal of Psychoanalysis, 63* (4): 449–456.

Kenrick, J., Lindsey, C., & Tollemache, L. (Eds.) (2006). *Creating New Families: Therapeutic Approaches to Fostering, Adoption, and Kinship Care.* London: Karnac.

Kernberg, O. (1975). *Borderline Conditions and Pathological Narcissism*. New York: Jason Aronson.

Kipling, R. (1894). *The Jungle Book*. Oxford Children's Classics. Oxford: Oxford University Press, 2007.

Klein, M. (1932). *The Psychoanalysis of Children*. London: Hogarth Press.

Klein, M. (1936). Weaning. In: *The Writings of Melanie Klein, Vol. 1: Love, Guilt and Reparation and Other Works 1921–1945* (pp. 290–305). London: Routledge.

Klein, M. (1937). Love, guilt and reparation. In: *The Writings of Melanie Klein, Vol. 1: Love, Guilt and Reparation and Other Works 1921–1945* (pp. 206–343). London: Routledge.

Klein, M. (1946). Notes on some schizoid mechanisms. In: *The Writings of Melanie Klein, Vol. 3: Envy and Gratitude and Other Works 1946–1963* (pp. 1–24). London: Routledge, 1975.

Klein, M. (1957). Envy and gratitude. In: *The Writings of Melanie Klein, Vol. 3: Envy and Gratitude and Other Works 1946–1963* (pp. 176–235). London: Routledge, 1975.

Klein, M. (1959). Our adult world and its roots in infancy. In: *The Writings of Melanie Klein, Vol. 3: Envy and Gratitude and Other Works 1946–1963* (pp. 247–263). London: Routledge, 1975.

Klein, M. (1975). *The Writings of Melanie Klein, Vol. 3: Envy and Gratitude and Other Works 1946–1963*. London: Routledge.

Kramer, K. I. (2015). Cooperative Breeding and human evolution. In: R. Scott & S. Kosslyn (Eds.), *Emerging Trends in the Social and Behavioral Sciences*. Wiley Online Library [doi: 10.1002/9781118900772].

Liotti, G. (1992). Disorganized/disoriented attachment in the etiology of the dissociative disorder. *Dissociation, 5*: 196–204.

Main, M., & Solomon, J. (1986). Discovery of an insecure-disorganised/disorientated pattern. In: T. Brazelton & Y. Yogman (Eds.), *Affective Development in Infancy* (pp. 95–124). Norwood, NJ: Ablex.

Mather, M. (2018). *Dealing with Foetal Alcohol Spectrum Disorder: A Guide for Social Workers*. CoramBAAF Good Practice Guide. London: Coram.

McDougall, J. (1978). Primitive communication and the use of countertransference. *Contemporary Psychoanalysis, 14*: 173–209.

Menzies, I. (1960). A case-study in the functioning of social systems as a defence against anxiety. *Human Relations, 13* (2): 95–121.

Midgley, N., & Vrouva, I. (Eds.) (2012). *Minding the Child: Mentalization-based Interventions with Children, Young People and Their Families*. London: Routledge.

Miller, A. (1981). *Prisoners of Childhood*. New York: Basic Books.

Music, G. (2017). *Nurturing Natures; Attachment and Children's Emotional, Sociocultural and Brain Development* (2nd edition). London: Routledge.

Novakovic, A. (Ed.) (2016). *Couple Dynamics: Psychoanalytic Perspectives in Work with the Individual, the Couple, and the Group*. London: Karnac.

Pereira Gray, D. J., Sidaway-Lee, K., White, E., Thorne, A., & Evans, P. H. (2018). Continuity of care with doctors—a matter of life and death? A systematic review of continuity of care and mortality. *BMJ Open, 8* (6).

Pullman, P. (1995). *His Dark Materials: Northern Lights*. London: Scholastic.

Pullman, P. (2000). *His Dark Materials: The Amber Spyglass*. London: Scholastic.

Rowling, J. K. (1998). *Harry Potter and the Chamber of Secrets*. London: Bloomsbury.

Roy, A. (2017). (with Thomas, C., & Simmonds, J.). *Adoption Support: Integrating Social Work and Therapeutic Services—the AdCAMHS Model*. Coram BAAF Briefing Paper. London: Coram.

Rustin, S. (2014). Edward Timpson: "I wouldn't be children's minister if my parents hadn't fostered". *The Guardian*, Family Section, 29 March. Available at: www.theguardian.com/lifeandstyle/2014/mar/29/edward-timpson-childrens-minister-parents-fostered

Salomonsson, B. (2014). Psychodynamic therapies with infants and parents: A review of RCTs on mother–infant psychoanalytic treatment and other techniques. *Psychodynamic Psychotherapy, 42* (4): 617–640.

Scharff, D., & Scharff, J. (2014). An overview of psychodynamic couple therapy. In: D. Scharff & J. Scharff (Eds.), *Psychoanalytic Couple Therapy* (pp. 3–24). London: Karnac.

Schore, A. N. (1994). *Affect Regulation and the Origin of the Self: The Neurobiology of Emotional Development*. Hillsdale, NJ: Lawrence Erlbaum.

Schore, A. N. (2000). Attachment and the regulation of the right brain. *Attachment & Human Development, 2* (1): 23–47.

Schore, A. N. (2001). Effects of a secure attachment relationship on right brain development, affect regulation and infant mental health. *Infant Mental Health Journal, 22*: 1–6.

Schore, A. N. (2003a). The human unconscious: The development of the right brain and its role in early emotional life. In: V. Green (Ed.), *Emotional Development in Psychoanalysis, Attachment Theory, and Neuroscience: Creating Connections* (pp. 23–54). London: Brunner-Routledge.

Schore, A. N. (2003b). Early relational trauma, disorganized attachment, and the development of a predisposition to violence. In: M. F. Solomon & D. J. Siegel (Eds.), *Healing Trauma: Attachment, Mind, Body, and Brain* (pp. 107–167). New York: Norton.

Schore, A. N. (2012). *The Science of the Art of Psychotherapy*. New York: Norton.

Selwyn, J., Wijedasa, D., & Meakings, S. (2014). *Beyond the Adoption Order: Challenges, Interventions and Adoption Disruption*. Research report, University of Bristol School for Policy Studies Hadley Centre for Adoption and Foster Care Studies. London: Department for Education.

Shedler, J. (2010). The efficacy of psychodynamic psychotherapy. *American Psychologist, 65* (2): 98–109.

Shelley, M. W. (1818). *Frankenstein; or, The Modern Prometheus*. London: Lackington, Hughes, Harding, Mavor, & Jones.

Siegel, D. J. (1999). *The Developing Mind: How Relationships and the Brain Interact to Shape Who We Are*. New York: Guilford Press.

Simmonds, J. (2008). Developing a curiosity about adoption. In: D. Hindle & G. Shulman (Eds.), *The Emotional Experience of Adoption: A Psychoanalytic Perspective* (pp. 27–41). London: Routledge.

Solomon, R. (2018). No shit! A psycho-educational group for foster carers. In: M. Bower & R. Solomon (Eds.), *What Social Workers Need to Know* (pp. 148–164). London: Routledge.

Sroufe, L. A. (2005). *The Development of the Person: The Minnesota Study of Risk and Adaptation from Birth to Adulthood*. New York: Guilford Press.

Steele, M., Hodges, J., Kaniuk, J., Hillman, S., & Henderson, K. (2003). Attachment representations and adoption: Associations between maternal states of mind and emotion narratives in previously maltreated children. *Journal of Child Psychotherapy, 29* (2).

Steele, H., & Steele, M. (2008). On the origins of reflective functioning. In: F. Busch (Ed.), *Mentalization: Theoretical Considerations, Research Findings, and Clinical Implications* (pp. 133–158). New York: Routledge.

Steiner, J. (1993). *Psychic Retreats: Pathological Organizations in Psychotic, Neurotic and Borderline Patients*. London: Routledge.

Steiner, J. (2011). *Seeing and Being Seen*. London: Routledge.

Stern, D. N. (1985). *The Interpersonal World of the Infant*. New York: Basic Books.

Stevenson, R. L. (1883). *Treasure Island*. London: Collins, 1953.

Teicher, M. H., & Samson, J. A. (2016). Annual Research Review: Enduring neurobiological effects of childhood abuse and neglect. *Journal of Child Psychology and Psychiatry, 57* (3): 241–266.

Triseliotis, J. (1973). *In Search of Origins: The Experience of Adopted People*. London: Routledge & Kegan Paul.

Triseliotis, J., Howe, D., Feast, J., & Kyle, F. (2005). *The Adoption Triangle Revisited: A Study of Adoption, Search and Reunion Experiences*. London: British Association for Adoption and Fostering.

Tronick, E., Adamson, L. B., Als, H., & Brazelton, T. B. (1975). *Infant Emotions in Normal and Perturbated Interactions*. Paper presented at the biennial meeting of the Society for Research in Child Development, Denver, CO (April).

Tyler May, E. (1988). *Homeward Bound: American Families in the Cold War Era*. New York: Basic Books, pp. 16–36.

van der Kolk, B. (2014). *The Body Keeps the Score: Brain, Mind, and Body in the Transformation of Trauma*. New York: Penguin.

Waddell, M. (1998). *Inside Lives: Psychoanalysis and the Growth of the Personality*. London: Duckworth.

Winnicott, D. W. (1945). Primitive emotional development. *International Journal of Psychoanalysis, 26*: 137–143.

Winnicott, D. W. (1953). Transitional objects and transitional phenomena: A study of the first not-me. *International Journal of Psychoanalysis, 34*: 89–97.

Winnicott, D. W. (1960). The theory of the parent–infant relationship. *International Journal of Psychoanalysis, 41*: 585–595.

Winnicott, D. W. (1963). Psychiatric disorders in terms of infant maturational processes. In: *The Maturational Processes and the Facilitating Environment* (pp. 230–241). London: Karnac, 1990.

Winnicott, D. W. (1967). Mirror-role of mother and family in child development. In: *Playing and Reality* (pp. 111–128). London: Routledge, 1971.

Winterson, J. (1985). *Oranges Are Not the Only Fruit.* New York: Grove Press, 1997.

Winterson, J. (2011). *Why Be Happy When You Could Be Normal?* London: Vintage, 2012.

INDEX